Table of Contents

UNDER THE MIGHTY HAND OF GOD!

Today there is a tremendous outpouring of God's Spirit all over the world. Recent gatherings have revealed unusual signs, restoration, sense of awe, and much more. Many ask is this the real thing or just great meetings. If this is not the real thing, it will do until the Real Thing arrives. Many ask, "How can we contain what God is doing." I Peter 5:6 tells us to, "humble yourselves under the mighty hand of God." I term this the Five Fold Hand of God.

The Five Fold Hand of God represents the ministry of Ephesians 4:11-12. The thumb represents the Apostle. His heart is for the overall vision of the organization and how to govern it. The thumb is the only one that can touch all the other fingers. The Apostle makes sure that all the gifts are speaking into the group, assuring that the total voice of Jesus is heard.

The index finger represents the Prophet. His heart is to point the way and help guide us into it. He is the spiritual thermometer and inspires creativity.

The tall middle finger represents the Evangelist. He is reaching out farther to the lost and hurting. His objective is to gather the harvest into one place.

The ring finger represents the Pastor. His heart is to guard the Sheep. He is more sensitive to wolves, sickness, hurts, and food than the other gifts.

The little finger represents the Teacher. Teachers ground us in the word of God. His love for the truth is enlightening for all that can receive. This is just a pictorial summary of these gifts. When all these gifts are received, recognized and released the people remain under the hand of God.

When the Five Fold Hand of God is restricted, the effect is detrimental for God's people trying to reach their destiny. Lamentations 5: 12 states, "Princes (five fold elders) were hung by the hands." Space will not permit complete insight, so I will just list some of the effects when the Five Fold is not recognized or severely restricted from a group.

Lamentations:

2: 8 "no restraining of God's hand from destroying." The very gifts God uses to build and equip, can destroy. How? People not receiving their instruction or counsel.

2: 9 "Gates (Authority) have sunk into the ground" representing broken down authority in the home, church, employment, and government.

2:10 "elders... they are silent..."no ability to rule or as 5:12 states, they are not respected.

2:11a "My spirit is greatly troubled..." lack of constant peace.

2:11b "little ones and infants faint..." v19 "faint because of hunger" the young are entertained with programs, events, or social fulfillment, yet their spiritual hunger is never satisfied.

2:13 "who can heal you..." people remain in spiritual, emotional, and physical sickness.

2:14 "Your prophets have seen for you False and Foolish visions..." They have NOT exposed, restored, but have seen false and misleading oracles.

Why? When people invest power in human heroes they give them power to prophesy out of themselves without checks and balances. The reason for not exposing is because the prophets themselves dwell in iniquity and are in captivity.

5:8 "Slaves rule over us. There is no one to deliver us from their hand."
Proverbs 30: 21-23 warns when a slave becomes a king, the earth quakes. Slaves have a master who controls their lives.

5:12-15 I will just list them: no respect for elders, heavy burdens on the young, youth constantly stumbling, elders have no authority, music is gone or replaced, joy has ceased, festive celebration has become mourning, and etc. etc. (I told you there is not enough room.)

To sustain what God is doing there must be restoration of the Five Fold Hand of God. Luke 6: 6-11, Jesus is teaching on the Sabbath. The crowd consisted of scribes, Pharisees, a man with a withered right hand and others. Several observations are crucial to the restoring of the Five Fold Hand of God. First, there will always be resistance from the ones who should know, but refuse to learn. Scribes and Pharisees are like some of our leaders today, the five fold gifts stand in front of them and they do not recognize it. Jesus Christ was the only one who had all gifts residing in Him. Second, leaders will always give a reason why these things are not for us. When we succumb to reason, it will manifest in accusation of those who are walking out a truth. Third, it says "that Jesus Christ knew their thoughts," An accusative heart will be known by many even without speaking a word. Fourth, the people of God must rise up to the ignorant lies that we have believed and take a stand for God's way. Fifth, when we take a stand it will cause us to stretch out and receive these gifts. Hebrews 9:10 talks about a "time of reformation" Reformation is the Greek word, *"deorthosis"* meaning: to straighten, making straight of what is out of line by coming of a drastic NEW order of reality. The Five Fold Hand of God will stretch us in every area of our lives. Enraging us and yet embracing us at the same time.

When the Five Fold Hand of God is restored it releases an outpouring of His Spirit. I Kings 17 tells of Elijah the Prophet confronting King Ahab. He prophecies that it would not rain for three and a half years and it happened. I Kings 18: 41-46 gives a wonderful picture of what happens when the Five Fold Hand of God is restored. It is now the end of three and half years of no rain. Elijah begins to intercede for rain. He sends his servant to see if rain was coming. He checks seven times, on the seventh time, he reports, "a cloud the size of a man's hand is coming up out of the sea." Notice what happens: the sky grew black, wind blew and a heavy rain fell. the servant had to go seven times signifying God's completion of the last prophetic word and the beginning of prophetic intercession. Then the Five Fold Hand of God begins to rise out of the sea; representing the masses of humanity. The servant saw the cloud like a MAN'S HAND. What was in that hand? Darkness covering the earth and the people, the wind of the Spirit, to blow away the chaff of ungodliness in His people, and the heavy rain being poured out on all. The Prophet then gives direction to governmental authority (King Ahab) to prepare, to humble himself or the outpouring will overtake them. Some will try to ride the outpouring on their own strength (chariots=man made machinery), while others will be running to the a new place in God. Notice where they went; "Jezreel." This name means, "God Sows." The new outpouring of His Spirit is a transition from the previous leadership to new ones. They will be planted by God Himself. Those flowing with the Five Fold Hand of God will remain in their proper place.

In conclusion, those who humble themselves under the mighty hand of God will have longevity and remain in this fresh outpouring today.

The Second Wind

In the 1990's a prophetic word came to the Body of Christ regarding two different Winds. The first wind would be named, "Holiness Unto the Lord." It describes the condition of the church and God's attitude and action toward it. The second wind is named, "The Kingdom of God." This wind will bring God's government, order, and power. This will release supernatural miracles and the fear of the Lord. Recent events and prophecies lead me to believe we are now moving into this second wind. This second wind will bring in an even greater harvest of souls. How are we to process this harvest? Who will God use in this process? What must change in order to help this process?

Nothing has been more detrimental to the Kingdom of God than the loss of the greatest labor force in all the world. We have substituted man's order for divine order, whereby both the gifts and ministries have largely ceased to function and believers have become SPECTATORS. In order to tap into this labor force we must change our thoughts and attitudes concerning the PROFESSIONAL CLERGY and THE LAITY.

The term "clergy" is never used in Scripture with reference to the five-fold ministry offices of Ephesians 4:11. The Greek term for "clergy" occurs only once in I Peter 5:3. In this passage the word speaks of the 'congregation of people'. Peter instructs the elders NOT to act as "lords over God's heritage." The term, "heritage" is the Greek word, *'KLEROS'* where we get "clergy". Later the elders came to consider themselves, like the Levites and the priests in the Old Testament, God's special, "heritage". Thus the clergy became 'professionals' in the field of Christianity. Frank Damazio gives an excellent progression of this way of thinking.

Since the   'clergy' = priesthood

and the   'priesthood' = a profession

and   'a profession = a professional

The results: CLERGY   =   A PROFESSIONAL

The term "laity" is from a Greek word, '*LAOS*', meaning "people". In I Peter 2:9, the "laity" are called the 'royal priesthood'. The scriptures designate ALL believers as God's 'clergy' and 'priesthood'. ALL believers have been set in the Body with a ministry to perform. Some are ministry gifts of leadership for equipping and leading. Others spread the Word of God and minister to the needs of the people. ALL understood their calling, regardless of their place of employment. Acts 8: 1-4 states that ordinary disciples or 'laity' were scattered abroad and "went every where preaching the word". The church today needs for each Christian to become full-time disciples, witnessing and ministering within the sphere of their life and employment. More on this in the Chapter "Apostolic Authority in the Local Church".

The function then of the five-fold ministry is to prepare His Body for its ministry and bring it to a place of maturity. How is this accomplished? Ephesians 4: 8-16 gives us some good insight.

Verse 8 states, "...and He gave gifts unto men..." In verse 11, Paul names these gifts. They are apostles, prophets, evangelists, teachers, and pastors. (For an in-depth description of these functions refer to earlier editions of SEEC Magazine.) These gifts are given in order for Jesus to, "FILL ALL THINGS." verse 10. He is the One who is to fill all things. The word, 'FILL' is from the Greek text, "*PLERAO* ". It has the idea of, "pervading or richly furnishing something with a substance". God's desire is to have Himself through Jesus Christ pervading and richly furnishing all things with the Glory of His presence. As God's presence and glory pervades the Church, God can cause His manifested glory to be known in the earth.

In order for the five-fold gifts to equip the saints and bring them, "...unto the measure of the stature of the FULLNESS OF CHRIST," (verse 13) then they must be filled up with all things in Christ. Out of this fullness there will come an impartation to the Church of what He is and thereby have Himself seen and known in the earth. The Kingdom of God must be in us, before it can be released out of us. No single individual, hierarchical system, or ecclesiastical ceremony has the ability to totally proclaim this to a particular single group. Thus, the five-fold ministries become the five-fold voice of Jesus Christ. (Hebrews 1:3) To have mature and well rounded people all the gifts must be speaking and functioning in the universal and local Church.

In this world wide harvest, God is restoring the apostolic expression [baptism in the Holy Spirit], the apostolic message [Christ's deliverance for the total man], the apostolic works [signs, wonders and miracles], the apostolic faith [trust and dependence on God and His promises]. His purpose is to produce APOSTOLIC CHRISTIANITY, whereby the Body of Christ will once again function as it did in the beginning.

The Second Wind is moving and God is truly preparing the Church for the harvest. It must be harvested and processed in the order that He prescribes. Let us take a wholesome look at the Church and prepare it.

"He Gave Some As Apostles"

Jesus said, "I will build My Church..." (Mt. 16:16-19) Jesus did nothing except for what he saw or heard the Father doing. Wanting to please the Father, he would build according to the Divine pattern. God's design or blueprint is clearly expressed throughout the Scriptures. When this design, blueprint or pattern was followed, God's abiding glory would remain and confirm that pattern. God only places His Glory on that which is according to His pattern. Jesus Christ is the Builder of the New Testament Church. He also called along co-laborers to build with Him, under His direction and supervision. Ephesians 4:8;11-13 tells us after Jesus descended in to hell, He ascended giving gifts unto mankind. These are five ministry gifts. Five is the number that God links with grace, atonement, and life. It is through these five gifts that the Lord reveals Himself in a physical way to the world. We will look at the Apostle's grace.

Apostle is a frightening word to many in the modern church. It has been misused, abused, and confusing to most of the church. Yet, we must recognize the need for apostolic ministry in our world today.

The definition of the words, "Apostolos" was taken from a secular term and expanded by the Church. In the Classical Greek world it meant: personal envoy, emissary or ambassador; fleet of ships or and expedition sent overseas. The Hebrew usage: "Shalach" is the equivalent to him who has sent him. Not a substitution, but the one who commissions is seen to be present in the person. The person is sent forth with authority and faithfully represents the purposes and the intentions of the sender. Jesus states, "The servant is not greater than his lord: neither he that is sent greater than he that sent him." (Jn. 13:16: Mt. 10:40) The Greek meaning for "Apostolos" is: "one who is sent forth."

There are 28 apostles mentioned in the New Testament. Fourteen are BEFORE

Pentecost: Jesus (Heb. 3:1) "The Apostle and High Priest of our confession." Rabbis applied the apostle to the priesthood and some prophets. (Isa. 6:8; I Kgs 14:6; II Kgs 19:4) The Twelve Apostles of the Lamb (Rev. 21:14) There are four listings of these twelve. Matthew 10:2-4; Mark 3:16-19: Luke 6:12-16; and Acts 1:26 . Each list mentions Peter first, and Judas the traitor last.

Fourteen are AFTER Pentecost: Paul, Barnabas, Apollos, Andronicus, Junia, Epaphroditus, Titus, two unnamed brothers in II Cor.8:23, Timothy, Judas, Silas, Eratus, Tychicus.

There is no proven evidence that this ministry gift has ever ceased. Even though the eminent apostles, or super apostles, or chiefest apostles (II Cor.11:5; 12:11 NAS) has ceased, there are still many missionaries and ministries in our day that do qualify according to Apostolic grace manifested in and through them.

Do all churches need an Apostle? No, but they all must be Apostolic in nature. This will include the apostle's ministry. Acts 13 reveals the role and characteristics of the "Apostle's" gift.

1. Planted in a local church. v.1 "... in the church..."

In the Old Testament many times the prophet was found out in the field and God would send a word for a group or situation. After the twelve are chosen by Jesus we then see the New Testament apostle coming from the church. This revealed how much Jesus and His body are one.

2. Commissioned v.2a "...set apart for me..."

In the New Testament, apostles were called, "masterbuilders." According to the grace of God which is given unto me, as a WISE MASTERBUILDER...   (I Cor.3:10) Masterbuilder is taken from the Greek word, "architekon" meaning an architect or a superintendent in erection of a building. Other root words mean a leader, first in a series, builder, joiner, or planner. The apostle is one who sees the Big Picture and is commissioned to:

    * Found and establish churches. If he went into an area where there was no church, he could start one. They are sometimes called the, "The father of the Work." The Hebrew word for, "Father" means, "Beginning."

    * Bring Illumination to Revelation and doctrine. Acts 2 talks about the Apostle's Doctrine. In the Old Testament the prophets wrote the progressive revelation of God's plan, but in the New Testament the apostles wrote the completed revelation of that plan.

    * Set up church government and to lay a foundation. (I Cor. 3:10-11) God has set in the church; governments (plural) = steering, piloting, and directing. Isaiah 9:6-9 "The government shall be on His shoulders." Isa. 22:22 "The government shall be placed in the hand of Eliakim." Eliakim means, "Resurrection of God" The foundation must be built upon the Rock; Jesus Christ. (Ephesians 2:20)

    * Organize Elders. Titus 1:5, I Timothy 3:1-9 This gives the explanation of what to look for in an elder, deacon, etc. This gives the basis for Biblical order in the church.

    * Delegate Authority I Timothy 1:18; 4:14: II Timothy 1:6 Authority is given not to bind, but to advance us.

    3. No Loners v 2b "... Barnabas and Paul..."

The book of Acts reveals that Apostolic teams worked together. No apostle was a Loner or independent of the other churches or ministry.

    4. the Work v. 2c "... the work to which I have called them..." Please notice that it is a WORK. The normal pattern: They would come into an area where there is no group or a young group was meeting, then they would start to help structure the group, stay until the appointing of leaders, then move on to the next place. To manage the WORK they usually supported themselves or received assistance from other churches. They would rent their own facilities and build from there. (Acts 28:30-31) Phillipians 1:1 shows the description of a New Testament church. When the group

had elders, deacons, and saints then it had become a church.

     5. Opposition v.8   "Elymas... withstood them..."

Spiritual Warfare is constant. It was Paul who suffered the greatest on the team, as he carried the revelation of Jesus Christ to the Gentiles. There was always a messenger of Satan to oppose him.

     6. Signs and Wonders vv. 9-12   "...The hand of the Lord be upon thee and thou shalt be blind...being astonished...." Signs and Wonders are a good indication of God's direction and sending.

     7. Trans Local ministry vv 13-14   "Paul and company....from Paphos...to Perga... to Antioch"   The cycle again was to establish a work until it became a church or had strong leadership.

The apostle and prophet have a greater burden for the universal church as well as the local church. The New Testament reveals two kinds of churches. First, the Local Church in a particular area or region. Such as: Lystra, Iconium, Derbe, etc. Second, the World Centers of propagating the gospel. These were launching places for ministry and the apostles, prophets, and teachers gave the oversight.

     8. Prophetic Preaching and Teaching vv 15-42

Paul would talk about the abundance of revelation he had received. (II Cor. 12:1-12) The purpose for this revelation was two-fold. One, to reveal God's will to the unknown. Second, to give indirect revelation by accepting an invitation to that group. (v.42)

     9. Persecution v,50   "the Jews stirred up...and raised persecution Persecution precedes entering. The reason; to realign a culture that has moved away from Godly principles. When realignment starts people will always REACT to the move back to those Godly principles.

     10. Great Influence v 52   "... disciples were filled with joy and with the Holy Ghost." The apostle must have influence in the group in order for church

discipline, to feed and equip. They will have influence over some, but not over all.

As with every ministry there will be the true and the false. The scriptures warn against false apostles. Revelation 2:2 tells us to try (test) those who SAY they are apostles, but are not. In order to test a false apostle, let us look at some characteristics found in II Cor. 11: 1-15.

- Deception v 3   Done through corrupting the mind.
- Preach another Jesus v 4a
- Different spirit v 4b
- Proclaim a different gospel v 4c
  Superior to proven ministries v 5   "chiefest" means people who wanted to be taken as super apostles, whose words prevail over and above the original twelve apostles.
- The motive is money vv 7-9
- Pride is the root   v 12 "... Wherein they glory"
- Fruit of their labor is Wrong Deeds v 15
- Bring people into Bondage v 20

Now we will recognize a true apostle. When we recognize the true, then we can receive them. To receive those who have been sent by the Lord is to receive the Lord who sent them. (Mt. 10:40; I Thes.4:8) There are four key areas to recognizing an Apostle.

- Apostle should know his grace gift.
- That grace gift should be recognized by the local church leadership.
- Apostle's gift is recognized by the People in his own church
- His gift should be recognized by those he has grounded and

established in the faith.

If a person has a tried and true apostolic ministry gift, then the church should receive such. Receiving then releases the Apostolic gift and the church receives the reward of that ministry's labor in the word of the Lord.

Finally, the goal of Apostolic Ministry is found in Colossians 1:27-28. To whom God willed to make known what is the riches of the glory of this mystery among the Gentiles which is Christ in you the hope of glory. 28 And we proclaim Him, admonishing every man and teaching every man with all wisdom, that we may present every man complete in Christ. Today we have struggling Christians trying to reach their potential in Christ. Maybe we should once again give greater attention to the role of the Apostle in the modern church. By accepting the apostle's role our foundation will be more sure and our walk with the Lord stronger.

<u>"And He Gave Some As Prophets!"</u>

Since the beginning God has been a God who speaks. Paul declares that God has "set" many gifts in the church, amongst these is the ministry of the Prophet. Since the outpouring of the Holy Spirit on the Day of Pentecost the prophetical sign was the confirmation of the beginning of the last days. (Joel 2:28-32; Acts 2:14-21) The prophetic continued throughout the early church, but had lost its place through the centuries. Paul gave us the assurance that the Prophet would continue <u>UNTIL</u> the church comes to the unity of the faith and maturity. As many gifts are being restored in the church, we find the need for the prophetic today. We will not attempt to examine Prophecy, the gift of prophecy, or the Spirit of prophecy, but will examine the ministry of the Prophet.

The prophet is a spokesman for God. The Hebraic concept, the prophets were to speak as God's mouthpiece. (Hosea 12:10; Hebrews 1:1-2) Hebrew words describing the Prophet whom was prophesying were: "to boil over like a hot spring or fountain; to bubble up, burst forth with violence; or to speak utterance in exalted and excited manner," by the Spirit of God.

In the Greek world in Paul's day, prophecies did not suggest something only spoken under inspiration. PLATO had set the tone by teaching two kinds of prophecy. One was Mantic prophecy, "the prophecy of inspiration." The one speaking was doing so under the constraint of the divine, they were possessed by a god and became the mouthpiece of the god. The other was the "prophecy of Interpretation," an acquired skill. The Prophet had the ability to interpret signs and omens by rational discernment. This was quite clearly seen at the Oracle of Delphi (near Corinth) in which the Pythia (the oracle, who was a woman) spoke in a state of ecstasy and the prophet who was to interpret the oracle's saying using rational discernment. (Dunn, Jesus, P228; TDNT Vol. VI, pp. 786-788)   The Church today makes this distinction, opting for the latter kind of prophecy defined by Plato. Thus prophecy becomes, "preaching,' the interpretation of the Bible. Thus the ministry of the Prophet is not needed in the Church today. The Greek word: "Propheteuo" indicates a two -fold nature. It means: FORTHTELLING = the prophet uses this realm to communicate the mind of God for the PRESENT. This is expressed through prophetic preaching or teaching.

The second word is, FORETELLING = the prophet speaks for God, communicating His mind for the FUTURE. This is expressed in the form of prediction based on the past and present.

Moses prophesied, "a Prophet like me from your midst, from your brethren. Him you shall hear... and the Lord said to me: I will raise up for them a Prophet like you from among their brethren, and will put My words in His mouth, and He shall speak to them all that I command Him. And it shall be that whoever will not hear My words, which He speaks in My name, I will require it of him." (Deut. 18:15;18-19) The Talmud declares, " that the Messiah must be the greatest of the future prophets, as being the nearest in spirit to our master Moses. Who was or is this great Prophet to come? Jesus Christ! Throughout the Gospels and Epistles many places confirmed Jesus was the Prophet, "like unto Moses." In comparing the life of Moses and Jesus Christ there are many elements and events that are very similar in both lives. (It would be good to do a comparison study on these two men.) Jesus Christ has now become the mouthpiece of God. (Heb. 1:2) He only spoke the things He saw and heard from the Father. (John 4:19; 12:49; 14:10-24; 17:8) Now the Holy Spirit takes the things He hears and gives them to us. (John 15:26; 16:13-15) When Jesus ascended on high, He gave gifts to men. One of those gifts is the Prophet.

Let us now examine the ministry of the New Testament Prophet. We will follow the pattern in II Kings 2: 1-15.

First, THE ATTRIBUTES OF A PROPHET

·   He is planted in the local Church. v. 2 "... went down to Bethel."

Bethel means the "House of Prayer." I Cor. 12:28 states, "...set in the church, first apostles, secondarily prophets..." Prayer is a major concern for the prophet. His sensitivity to the spirit realm reveals the lack of or direction for prayer. Being planted in the local church gives them the spiritual covering and authority to speak what the Spirit is saying to the Churches. Acts 13: 1-4, "And there were at Antioch, ...IN THE CHURCH, prophets and teachers." Notice their importance: they ministered to the Lord, fasting, Holy Spirit spoke, (How? probably through the gift of prophecy) they laid hands on them, (Prophet probably confirmed the word received) they sent (gave authority) to them to go out. When the Prophets are received in the church, people are challenged in worship, prayer and fasting, manifestation of the gifts, and commissioning of their call.

·   Various Prophets v. 3 "...sons of the prophets."

As one of the ministry gifts of Ephesians 4, the prophet is also used to EQUIP the saints for the work of ministry. The Old Testament gives us insight of the importance of equipping. Schools of the Prophets were established for educational purposes and instruction pertaining to the Law of Moses. The primary focus of these schools was to maintain the spirit of the Law. Prophets were recognized in many ways: Seers, (I Sam. 9:9) Messengers, (Isa. 42:19) Interpreters or teachers, (Isa. 43:27) Visionary, (Ezekiel,

Daniel, Zechariah) Verbal, (Micah, Isaiah) Trance, (Daniel, Abraham, John the Revelator) Writers, and Non-writers.

·   Revelation v. 3 "... knowest thou...yes, I know."

As noted before prophecy is forthtelling, present situation, and foretelling, pertaining to the future. The prophet is one who walks with revelation for the present and the future. He will have revelation in such areas as: The word of God, problems of people, (Acts 21: 10-11 gives details of Agabus demonstrating and explaining to Paul how he was going to Jerusalem and what will happen to him) another area is in regards to future events. (Acts 11:27-28 Agabus gives a predictive word about the coming famine.) Please note that in the Old Testament the prophets wrote as they were MOVED, inspired, illuminated by the Holy Spirit. (II Peter 1:20-21) They were not giving their own opinion, but rather the word given by God.

·   Loyalty v. 4 "...please stay here...I will not leave you."

I Samuel 12: 1-15 Nathan the Prophet comes to King David with a word from the Lord in regards to David's sin with Bathsheba. Notice verse 15, "So Nathan went to his house." Many prophets today wait to see if their word will be accepted and if not they move on to the next place, believing that the group will not change, but remain in its sin or predicament. This was not so in Biblical days, they remained loyal to help bring the word to pass, unless otherwise instructed by God. They helped nurture, encourage, and remind people of God's word. Many remained faithful to the Community. Constantly running from place to place is sign of immaturity, but being loyal reveals the maturing of the prophet. Much more could be shared in this area.

• Submissive v. 5 "...your master from over you."

Submission deals with the attitude of the heart. Prophets are not afraid to have their words or actions tested. In fact, they wait many times for other prophets or gifts to give the word and then come with the confirmation. A true prophet is subject to the prophets. III John 9-10 describes a man by the name of Diotrephes who lacked a submissive heart.

• Work with Others v. 6 "...two of them went on."

The prophet works with the Apostle to lay a foundation in the church. I have worked with Prophets in several events and seen the hand of God do some mighty powerful work. Confirmation of the churches is done through a team. Acts 15:32,41 shows how the team strengthened and encouraged the church with lengthy messages. Acts 13:1-4, we see prophets and teachers giving the word to the gathering and from there they sent out ministries. The team concept is continually seen throughout scripture.

Second, BENEFITS OF THE PROPHET

• Miracles vv. 7-8 "took the mantle ...struck the ground...dry ground"

Many prophets demonstrated and performed miracles. Miracles were used many times as confirmation of the call of God.

• Anointing v. 9 "...let a double portion of your spirit."

It was obvious to Elisha that the spirit rested upon Elijah. Receiving a double portion would confirm his role as the successor, heir or even first born birthright. The anointing publicly authorized a man's leadership. It set him apart for service to the Lord and gave him divine strength to carry out his work. Up until this time Elisha had the anointing WITHIN, now he was ready for service and needed the anointing UPON him and it must continue to increase. The anointing destroys the yokes of bondage that people have been entrapped under. I John 2:27 implies an anointing that we receive for ministry gifting.

· Predictive v. 10 "...If you see me..."

When a Jewish son had come of age, his father would acknowledge the son by saying, "This now is my full, recognized son." Then the father would give the KEYS to his estate, name, wealth, power, and seal. The son had full use to anything that belonged to the father. Elijah speaks prophetically to Elisha and says these words in order for him to have everything plus much, much more. The prophet declares what our Father has given to us. Thereby placing the KEYS in our hands to what God's future holds for us. If we will use those KEYS, God will be glorified and our lives enriched. The prophet only prophecies in part and each word we receive and act upon, gives us another KEY to the ultimate picture God has painted for us.

I must add here that Old Testament Prophets were used in GUIDANCE, DIRECTION, AND expressing the MIND AND WILL OF GOD. They also spoke and wrote the Old Testament Scriptures. The focus in the Old Testament is the PROPHET. The New Testament Prophets are used for confirmation of already known and revealed will of God. They are also used to WARN of impending danger, wrong direction, or information. The major focus in the New Testament is the PROPHECY.

•   Encouragement vv. 11-12 "... going along and talking..."

The prophet's words are used to effect eight main areas:

1. Edification - To build up or strengthen, the process of building or putting together. Because we go through so many difficult seasons in our walk, God sends the prophet to edify us and the church. Our authority should be used for building up and not for destroying. (II Cor. 10:8)

2.   Exhortation - To encourage those under pressure; to call someone to your side for the purpose of strengthening; speaking good words. The Hebrew officers would do this before a battle. They would remind the soldiers of the past victories or the word of the Lord to them.

3.   Comfort - To speak to someone; keeping watch over someone by remaining close to them; to speak a warning; of   danger, or of doing something that will cause them harm; chastisement.

4.   Revelation - To impart, declare, make manifest, disclose; an uncovering. The idea of removing the lid from a jar and pouring something in.

5.   Knowledge - To bring understanding that causes a person to enter into the truth being taught, causing the person to adjust a way of thinking which results in strong convictions.

6.   Prophesying - Divine inspiration to declare the mind of God in any given situation, to affirm something beforehand.

7.   Doctrine - Teaching, clear instruction given so as to establish the instruction as a way of thinking and living.

8.   Conviction - Idea of someone opening themselves up as a result of the word given to them.

Third, CALL OF THE PROPHET

·	Consents to the office v. 13 "He took up the mantle..."

The prophet must know that he has a distinct calling from God. Many mantles are still laying on the ground today because of ignorance, non-acceptance, or wrong belief about the prophet. If your grace is to be a prophet, I implore you today to go out and pick up your mantle. If it does not fit, God will grow you into it

·	Confirmation of the office v. 14 "Where is the Lord, the God of Elijah? ...he struck the waters ... they were divided.

God has many ways to confirm His call on our lives. John sent his disciples to see if Jesus was the Messiah. When they asked Him the question, He answered and said to them, "Go and report to John what you have seen and heard: the blind receive their sight, the lame walk, the lepers are cleansed, and deaf hear, the dead are raised up, and the poor have the gospel preached to them. If you are called to this office then begin to function and God will confirm that gift.

·	Confirmation by others v. 15 "They said..."

Acts 15: 22,25,32 shows that the prophets were recognized by the leaders at the Jerusalem Church. These men were leaders. Their prophetic gift had been exercised in the local church and they were given the responsibility to go and share with the rest of the churches. Another confirmation is that a prophet is not received in his own country. (Mt. 13:57) Why? The old expression, "Familiarity breeds contentment." is often the struggle of people seeing you in a different light. Many of the great leaders were sent back to their homeland or town, not only for the people, but so that God can do the preparatory work for a greater mission in the future.

II Chronicles 20:20 states, "Believe My prophets and you will succeed." Let's get 20/20 vision today and embrace the Prophets in the land.

Apostle & Prophet Laying the Foundation

Ephesians 2:19-22 "So then you are no longer strangers and aliens, but you are fellow citizens with the saints, and are of God's household, having been built upon the foundation of the apostles and prophets, Christ Jesus Himself being the cornerstone, in whom the whole building being fitted together is growing into a holy temple in the Lord; in whom, you also are being built together into a dwelling of God in the Spirit."

Have you ever watched the construction of some of the huge skyscrapers in our major cities? How do they stand so tall without falling over? What makes them so stable against the weather elements, high velocity winds and other major obstacles? Why do people feel safe and secure working on the top floors of such a massive structure? The answer is simple: "STRONG FOUNDATION!" The higher the structure goes, the deeper the foundation. While this is not an article on construction, it will address the needs in many Christians today and why the Apostle and Prophet are needed.

Due to the neglect of the apostolic and prophetic ministry in the church, much of the foundations are built on sand. Therefore, homes are crumbling, weak believers, unstable churches, and church division. Psalms 11:3 states, "If the foundations are destroyed, what can the righteous do?" There are many attacks on Biblical foundations today. Evolution, religion, education, psychiatry, etc. have invaded the church and believers to destroy their foundation. Jesus addresses lawyers (law-givers) in Luke 11:45-52. He is correcting them for the heavy rules and regulations they had placed on the people and pointed out that they have the same attitude as their forefathers, implying their agreement to kill the prophets. Verse 52, he brings a final indictment against them by stating, "you have taken away the key of knowledge, you did not enter in yourselves and those who were entering in, you hindered." The key of knowledge is a key placed in our hands to build a solid foundation, but this had been taken away. Verse 49 gives us God's wisdom of His future plan. He will send to them, prophets and apostles. They are the major foundation builders. Without a foundation, the church cannot stand the floods that will come against us in these last days.

This is why Jesus Christ warns that apostles and prophets would be killed and some would be driven out. The enemy does not want you to have a foundation to build your house.

Mat. 16: 16-18 states, "And Simon Peter answered and said, Thou art the Christ the Son of the Living God. And Jesus answered and said unto him, Blessed art thou, Simon Barjona: for flesh and blood hath not revealed it unto thee, but my Father which is heaven. And I say also unto thee, that thou art Peter, and upon this rock I will build my Church and the gates of hell shall not prevail against it."

Peter's confession gives us some insight to how Jesus would build His church. Many have tried to make Peter the issue in this particular passage, but later Jesus rebukes any that tried to usurp a place of autonomous authority. The focal point of this passage is the word. "REVEALED." The Father gives us revelation of Jesus. Revelation does not come by human effort or man's preconceived ideas, but rather by the Father. Revelation is the ROCK that He will build His Church, beginning with the foundation. The foundation must be built on a solid ROCK. The Greek word for "rock" is clearly a reference to Christ. (Rom 9:33; I Cor 10:4; I Ptr 2:7-8) Isaiah prophesies in Isaiah 28:16, of One who would come, upon whom we could build our lives. "Thus says the Lord God: Behold, I lay in Zion a stone for a foundation, a tried stone, a precious cornerstone, a sure foundation..." Paul clearly confirms that Christ is this sure foundation. (I Cor 3:11) The twelve apostles continually taught to root and ground the church in the doctrines of Christ. (Heb 6:1-2) If the Church is built on anything but Christ it is doomed to fall. We are living in a day when everything that can be shaken will be shaken. If we are built on Christ, if we are rooted and built up in Him, we will not be shaken nor will we fall. (Heb 13:9)

Now, Ephesians tells us that the Prophets and Apostles worked together to build this foundation. Each one has authority, but yet is distinct in its function to accomplish this task. Let us compare each role.

1.   The Revelation of God's Word

The Prophet received divine revelation from God, that was still in progress. Today, the prophet will prophesy in part of the revelation they received. I Cor 13: 9 states, "We prophecy in part....". This is why the prophet comes in and speaks progressive insight for the group.

The Apostle received the completed revelation. The 12 apostles of the Lamb gave the final approval of all written scripture. Now, the apostolic are sent with authority to establish and ground a particular group.

2.   Revelation came through Jesus Christ

Both the prophet and apostle are called the bond-servants of Jesus Christ, but all canon written needed apostolic approval.

Today, the prophet comes to confront the spiritual condition of the group.

The apostle confronts the soulish nature of the group.

The prophet releases the Spirit of the Lord and the apostle releases the Spirit of Truth.

3. Revelation's Two levels of Authority

The Bible implies a high and lower level of authority. We must understand these levels in order not to be confused between the two.

    * <u>For the Prophet:</u>

The higher revelation was manifested as he "spoke the Word for God". (Heb 1:1)

The lower revelation is manifested today, through edification, exhortation, or comfort. I Cor 14:2

Even though this is done through speaking, it is not the same as the higher level.

    * <u>For the Apostle:</u> The Twelve Apostles of the Lamb

Acts 1:21-22 states the three things to qualify as Apostle of the Lamb.

(1) Historical witness of Christ

(2) Historical witness of Resurrection and Ascension of Christ.

(3) Knew Christ Personally

The higher revelation came directly from God. (Gal 1:1)

The lower revelation is described as a Spirit of revelation. (Eph 1:17-18).

This Spirit of revelation is better described as; "illumination of the revelation" we already have from God's word.

In laying the right foundation, the apostle and prophet help us keep the following perspectives in focus.

* Since completion of Scripture, the level of authority in prophecy is lower then scripture. Gal 4:1-4

* Once revelation (illumination) is received, it must be tested. I John 4:1-5

* Ministry of the apostle came at the time of the full revelation of God in His Son.   Matt 5:17-19. This closed the Prophetic Age and the Apostolic Age began.

* Completion of scripture is marked by revelation of the Son of God. John 1:18.

* Bringing the body into maturity is accomplished through the ministry of the prophet in the Old Testament and apostles in the New Testament. These ministry gifts have not stopped and are still in the church today. I Cor 12:28

* The apostle's approval was the primary test for the New Testament Canon. Acts 6:4

* Only one who speaks in the New Testament with an authority that is NOT GIVEN is the Father.

* Error comes when revelation or prophecy are allowed to come to the level of the Bible in Authority.

God wants to lay that SURE foundation in His New Testament Church. A sure foundation is costly, but it will enable the building to stand in spite of the storms that may come. Embracing the prophet and apostle begin the process of construction for a solid and fruitful life. This will allow us to stand strong through any test and storm. " The firm foundation of God stands, having this seal, THE LORD KNOWS THOSE WHO ARE HIS. . . . ". II Tim. 2: 19

Apostolic Authority in the Local Church

When we look into the New Testament we see the five-fold gifts working together in harmony to bring the churches into a place of maturity. When the five-fold gifts are utilized and recognized the concept of victory begins to grasp and challenge the people. Today we have evolved into a place for the centrality of one-man with all the truth.

The Pastor has become the only voice to the people. In many gatherings people feel like the life-jackets are being thrown out to help them survive and not get a sense of conquering. If he grows, they grow and vice-versa. What has happened to the other functioning offices in the Church?

Apostolic Authority comes with a ZERO TOLERANCE mindset. They come in with all of the tools and begin to tighten things down that have become very loose. In establishing apostolic authority in the Local Church, let us examine some problems and understand God's principles, so that we might know our place.

In his book, 'The Making of a Leader', Frank Damazio explains how we transitioned from a plural leadership team to a single man concept. *The word 'authorization' is defined as the, 'state or quality of being given official authority or power to perform a duly sanctioned function.' The word 'authorization' comes from a Middle Latin word, 'auctorizare' which means , 'to increase or to grow.' The person who has received a true authorization from the Lord and not from man, is the person who has been anointed by God and is able to cause spiritual increase and growth in other people's lives.*

The Latin word, 'auctor' is the root of auctorizare, when interpreted with spiritual meanings it includes:

> 1. *a progenitor of spiritual families;*
> 2. *a builder of spiritual buildings;*

3.	*an author of spiritual writings;*

4.	*a doer of spiritual deeds;*

5.	*a teacher of spiritual knowledge;*

6.	*an informant of spiritual good news;*

7.	*a spiritual advisor of actions;*

8.	*a promoter of spiritual measures;*

9.	*a supporter of spiritual laws;*

10.	*a spiritual leader in public life;*

11.	*a model of spiritual conduct;*

12.	*a witness to spiritual promises;*

13.	*a spiritual guardian of women and minors;*

14.	*a champion of others' spiritual welfare.*

(Authorization of Ministry by Frank Damazio)

When this kind of fruit is obvious, this person has received authority to minister full-time.

Now that we have some understanding of authority, let's look at some reasons why the local Pastor has been placed in an awkward position.

<u>First</u>, the church felt that she could more easily stem the tide of IMMORALITY and INTELLECTUALISM with giving more power to one man. <u>Secondly</u>, the church believed that he could accomplish a greater unity against divisive heresies if she exalted certain strong teachers. <u>Thirdly</u>, the church began to use one man from each local assembly to represent them to the bishops of other local assemblies, which gradually led to the exaltation of this one man over the other local elders as the "episcopus par excellence". <u>Fourthly</u>, the church began to desire to financially support certain local leaders so that they could give all their time to ministering to the people. This brought about the idea that ministers/clergy were

considered the 'Professionals'. The word 'clergy' comes from the Latin and means 'clerk' and the ecclesiastical Latin word is 'clerius', meaning 'priest'. Thus, clergy = priesthood. The word 'profession' is the group of people engaged in a particular occupation or calling. Profession comes from the Latin word, 'professio' originally meaning "the taking of vows of a particular religious order." To became a priest they made a certain verbal profession of vows. Thus, priesthood = profession. The word 'professional' is described as a person who follows a specific occupation or renders a specific kind of service as a means of financial support. The words 'profession' and 'professional' applied to people fully engaged in any specific business activity for profit. Through this professing, the group or person understood the ideals for which their business stood. Thus, profession = professional. This gives us the progression of the 'Professional Clergy'.

Clergy = Priesthood

Priesthood = Profession

Profession = Professional

Therefore: Clergy = Professional

The culmination of this attitude began to politically separate certain men who desired position and prestige. <u>Fifthly</u>, the church began to desire to have most of the work of the ministry performed by the local leaders because they probably had the most education, which led to mainly the leader being in charge of education, doctrine, marriages, baptisms, the communion table, the elders, the deacons, and even church property and monies. Thus, the Priest was the specialist in the religious field and the layman was to serve as the representative to the secular world and run the business. This separation brought about a sense of continual 'DEFEATISM' in the church. If hope for victory is limited, then concern will be drastically narrowed. Therefore, any army/church which lacks confidence is defeated before it takes the field. <u>Sixthly</u>, the church began to look mainly to the local leader for all major teaching, and the local *elders were considered only 'teachers'; whereas the local priest was considered the joint Apostle/Prophet. [the true trans-local ministries of separate apostle and prophets having receded into the background.]*

The bishops/Senior leader supremacy can be accurately seen in the way that Ignatius of Antioch referred to the bishop. Ignatius commented, "We ought to regard the Bishop as the LORD himself". Consequently, the church digressed into the bishops being considered the apostles, prophets, and evangelists; the local elders being the pastors and teachers; the deacons mainly serving the bishops and the elders; the congregational members as being just "not in the ministry" of the Lord.

Matthew 22:14 states, "Many are called, but few are chosen." The necessity of a divine call begins to establish the authority of God. There are three basic ways that a man can be appointed to the place of authority.

<u>*Self-Appointed*</u>. The example in Numbers 16 & 17 of Korah, gives the characteristics of a self-appointed person.

1. He caused others to rise up.   v. 16:2
2. Publicly criticized existing leader. v. 16:3
3. Accused leaders of what he was found guilty of himself.   v.16:3
4. Not satisfied with his position, wanted more authority and higher position. v. 16:10
5. Continually murmured against the leader.   v.16:11

<u>*Man-Appointed*</u>.   The example in I Samuel 8:1-6; 11-17 of Israel's desire for a King. God warns them of the consequences. The Key phrase is, <u>"He Will Take!"</u>

1. Claim to receive a call from God.
2. Very common in our society.
3. Looks toward the ministry as a professional career.

God-Appointed. People who are appointed by God to function in a given capacity.

1. 'Appoint' Heb. - to oversee, to care for, to watch over.
II Samuel 6:21, Numbers 27:16,19,22; Acts 6:3

2. 'Separated' Heb. - set off by boundaries, to appoint, to set aside. Boundaries determine our anointing and faith.
I Chronicles 23:13, Romans 1:1, Acts 13:2

3. 'Called' Heb. - to accost a person, to call out by name, to summon.
Exodus 3:4, Romans 1:1, Acts 13:2, Mark 1:20

4. 'Sent' Heb. - to send away for specific reason.
Exodus 3: 12-18, Luke 4: 18, John 1:6

Once God's appointed person is in place the next question is, what authority structure needs to be established? The church is an autonomous entity that was created in the heart of God. Autonomy is, "having the right or power of self-government; undertaken or carried on without outside control." Therefore, the local church is identified in three distinguished areas. *First* the local church is to be SELF-GOVERNING. God has given a pattern for government. In the church, God refers to 'those who rule' or 'he that ruleth', or 'them that have the rule'. [I Timothy 5:17, Romans 12:8, Hebrews 13: 17,24] Rule means, "to be over, to superintend, to preside over, to care for, and to give attention to." All rulers must meet certain qualifications.

Second, the local church is, SELF-SUPPORTING. Through tithing, offerings, and alms the church is to meet all its spiritual, emotional and physical needs. Financial support is a sign of our personal relationship with God. When the children of Israel were in a backslidden state, a sign was the Levites had to pursue secular employment.

[Nehemiah 13: 10-12, Malachi 1: 7-14] A sign of revival was the restoration of God's economic system. [II Chronicles 31: 5-12]

Third, the local church is SELF-PROPAGATING.

Genesis 1: 28 was the first commandment to mankind. Jesus reiterates this again in Mark 16:15, when He charged all of us to, "Go Ye..." It is only as the church accepts a vision for training and equipping of its constituency, will there be a surfacing of ministry and thrusting out into the harvest field. For this reason each local church should support and maintain Christian education for its young people. Each local church should support and maintain a training program for prospective ministries. Each local church should encourage and be willing to make sacrifices to fulfill the commission set before the church. Often times this will mean sacrificing their very best for the furtherance of the Gospel of Christ.

Acts 13:1-4 gives us a great picture of this principle. In this passage we see the calling of Barnabas and Paul. When the decision was finalized, the two men were set apart for, "the WORK to which the Holy Ghost had called them..." Many have tried to centralize the government of the church in such places as: Jerusalem, Antioch, Ephesus, Rome, etc. Which raises some questions to consider. Did the leaders at Antioch feel a responsibility to oversee the ministry of these two Apostles? Did they feel that they were, "OVER" the churches that Paul and Barnabas planted? When the Antioch Church commended those men to God's grace, they acknowledged their qualifications and preparedness to embark on the mission. Through this commendation the leaders were acknowledging that the work of these two men was a trans-local ministry and out of their jurisdiction. Along with the apostolic work, all the five-fold gifts, that have maturity and experience, qualified to operate trans-locally and to live by the Gospel, and should be respected in that function. It was unseemly for a local church to feel that they had to be 'OVER' any church or ministry.

Now, we will look at the characteristics of "the work" in which they had been called. *First,* if there was no church in the area they had authority to establish one. *Second,* if there was a church in an area, they would go and build up that local assembly. *Third*, they worked among a specific target group. (i.e. Gentiles) *Fourth,* they would try to work within the established structure. They would go to the synagogue first. *Fifth*, if there was no response or work for the gospel they would: Start a Work - Manage it - Support it - Ordain Leaders - Move On.

II Corinthians 10: 8 states, "...about our authority, which the Lord gave for building you up and not for destroying you,..." Paul used his authority in a very constructive manner. He did not overstep that authority, but understood the limits and yet his realm in the local church. II Corinthians 10: 13 reads, "But we will not boast of things without our measure, but according to the MEASURE OF THE RULE which God has distributed to us, a measure to reach even unto you." This word 'rule' is taken from the Greek and is the same as our English word 'canon'. It literally means a straight rod and by its usage means a sphere of action or influence. The Japanese Bible expresses 'rule' as a <u>sphere of influence which is limited</u>. Paul shows his sphere of limited influence by stating, "a measure to reach even unto you..." reminding them of his fatherly oversight. The measure of rule is a concept in which Christ expresses His government through anointed individuals. Now we will conclude by looking at some areas of apostolic authority in the local church.

1.   Like a father to a married son. I Corinthians 4: 14-16

        This is more of an advisory role for the apostle.

2.   To teach doctrine. Especially, when it effects new works.

    Acts 2:42; 15: 1-31, I Corinthians 1: 10-11

    This is illustrated in Acts 6: 2-7

    Problem with feeding of the widows and serving tables.

    Not only was the physical threatened, but also the spiritual. They

    needed food, but the apostles needed   fresh revelation of the word for God's people. The result: widows needs were met and the Word of God increased.

3.   To assist in church discipline.

Acts 5: 1-11, I Corinthians 5

This was true, particularly to churches that looked to them for oversight or had been founded by the apostle. The apostle did not impose his authority on any church for discipline. He only came in when the local leadership invited him into the situation. Then discipline was administered usually on the issue that the majority agreed on.

4.   Assist in setting things in biblical order.

Elders and Deacons   Acts 6: 1-6; 14: 21, Titus 1:5

Presbytery   I Timothy 1: 18; 4: 14, II Timothy 1: 6

The apostle understood that proper biblical order did not bind the group, but it would advance the group into the ultimate purposes of God. Proper biblical order makes people accountable and responsible. It also helps to keep priorities in the right arrangements.

5.   Warning the churches of particular destructive individuals.

Galatians 1: 6, II John 6-11, III John 9-12

6.   On-going training for leadership.   Acts 28: 30-31

Time and time again you read the words in the book of Acts. "Let us go and CONFIRM, (STRENGTHEN, ENCOURAGE, BUILD UP) the brethren."

The apostle understood the key to perpetuating the gospel was to have good and qualified leaders. He also had the greatest burden in this area.

7.   Help with clarifying the vision.

8.	He also served as the set man where much ministry was being launched.	Acts 15

This is by no means a complete list for apostolic authority.

HANDLING THE PROPHETIC IN OUR MIDST

Several years ago I was sitting at a restaurant table with a group of Mexican pastors. Our fellowship was rich and enjoyable as we shared ghost stories---Holy Ghost stories. One story that remained with me through the years was about a small village church. The young pastor had been teaching for weeks on the Gifts of the Spirit. Wanting his people to use these gifts, he kept encouraging them to move out as the Spirit directed. No one seemed brave enough to step out. Frustrated, the pastor kept persisting and instructing. Finally one Sunday, during the worship service, a lady stood and began to prophesy. She blurted out the following, "Thus saith the Lord, . . . as MOSES was preparing to get into the ARK . . . " Upon completion, she then quietly sat down at the completion of her discourse. Suddenly, she jumped to her feet and yelled out again, "Thus saith the Lord, I made a mistake, it was not Moses. It was ABRAHAM." Whether this is a true story or not is irrelevant, but the fact remains that the prophetic brings out all kinds of things and situations.

Spiritual churches attract the prophetic type. The main reason, whether real or imagined, is the prophetic type person, who believe they are carrying a specific message for God. Some prophetic types in our midst are not normal and usually disruptive. It would be easy if they would come in with locust breath, camel suits, and yelling "a generation of vipers"! Then, we would know how to avoid or tolerate their unusual expressions or demonstrations. How do we live with these "want to be" prophets, prophesiers, or just spiritual weirdos?

The following principles will help serve as guidelines for us, while living with theses children of God.

(1)   <u>Accept every person sent to the Body</u>. Our basic tendency is not to like those who are not like us. Churches are no different than other social groups, becoming very cliquish in nature. We love all, but only relate to a few. This keeps us in our comfort zone. If someone invades that zone, our reaction is negative. When the prophetic come in we keep them at arms length in order to keep from be exposed. Realize the prophetic really loves God, even though they may have different perspectives about the church, harvest, interpretations, etc. Acceptance of people does not mean we have to agree with them. It allows us to lay ground work for all different kinds in the Body.

(2)   <u>The prophetic usually have Old Testament style with a New Testament ministry</u>. These are usually loners, intense and single-minded. When you get around the prophetic type, most everything is serious and a feeling of uptight. They live with a scowl on their face. The main reason is that the prophetic have a sensitivity to sin and are always harder on themselves. They try to live up to the message they are carrying. When they are unable to communicate the message or not live up to their call, they will get out of the ministry, doubt their call and battle depression.

(3)   <u>Listen to their Spirit FIRST, then listen to their words</u>. I Cor 14:29 instructs us that all prophesy must be judged. I have heard many beautiful words expressed and wonderful descriptive visions given during the prophetic flow. Romans 8:16 state, "The Spirit Himself bears witness with our spirit . . . " Listen to your spirit. The Spirit of God is not afraid to be tested or judged and is not in a hurry.

(4)   <u>Looks, attitude, behavior or gender are NOT determining factors of the Prophetic.</u> Many times we do not receive the gift because of how the package is wrapped. Confusion comes when we focus on the gift and overlook character traits. I

remember a time when I was leading a traveling group and we were at the verge of a crucial decision. At the conclusion of a group prayer meeting, a woman came in (whom we all named "Sally Spiritual") and said, "The Lord says, now is NOT the time." She turned around and left. If I would have rejected the person and the gift, we would have made a serious mistake in our decision.

(5)   <u>Delivery of the Prophetic is not important</u>. Different people have different presentations. Some are hard, some contradictory, some soft, some read their word, some visual, etc. I have met some who see things in the Spirit realm, but do not know how to express it. They seem to be a negative person.

(6)   <u>Judge each message by itself</u>. Not every prophetic person hits a home run all the time. They do prophesy in part. Each part leads to the whole. Do not put a part in where it does not belong. Discern when prophesy ends and exhortation begins. I have heard and spoken prophetically for many years. It still is a struggle to know when prophecy ends and then, out of desire to see people victorious, I begin to exhort them.

(7)   <u>Don't get defensive</u>. The prophetic may touch our pet truths, lifestyle, or belief system. Many times the word comes to shed more light on our present truths. The word will also sharpen us. It solidifies some of the things we believe or some areas we need to change.

(8)   <u>Understand our role</u>. Leaders are to protect and expose us to the voice of God. God will use strange and unexpected sources to stretch us. Sometimes they are too strange and fat out. Leaders must protect from error. The prophetic is a vulnerable area for many voices. The key is to warn, but people will listen to what they

want to hear. We are not the Lord, just a servant. So, remember, we do not tell people what to watch on T.V., what to read or what kind of entertainment to enjoy! All we can do is warn.

(9)   <u>Know the strength of your authority</u>. John 10 talks about the "voices of the Shepherd". Even thought the prophetic voice is valuable, remember as a spiritual authority your voice is final. Be secure in your role and call as Spiritual authority. When you know your authority, you can allow things to flow.

(10)   <u>Protect both people and the prophet</u>. In the Old Testament, the prophets operated in a solo mode. They received ridicule, were persecuted for their stand, and killed for their confrontation. In the New Testament, the emphasis is on a team concept. We find a submission of the prophetic to other leaders. This produces a protection for both the receivers of and the givers of the prophetic.

I must reiterate that these are some basic guidelines for receiving the prophetic types in our midst. By following these guidelines, we will be able to enjoy all kinds of the prophetic.

AND HE GAVE SOME AS EVANGELIST

Today we want to look at an important grace to the five-fold gifts that many are very familiar with the term, but not the function of the EVANGELIST. Our definitions run from the person handing out tracts on the streets, to the man with the wild clothes, who comes to our church once a year, to rant and rave about how lost we all are. Yes, we have been exposed to this more common title, but what does the EVANGELIST really mean and what is his or her function?

The Evangelist primary purpose is a preliminary ministry. Mel Cooley states in his book, <u>The Increases of His Government</u>. "The evangelist ministry is one of spiritual excavation, a clearing the ground in preparation for the building of the church, a GATHERING of stones with which to build. It is said we, '... as lively stones are built up a spiritual house...' (I Peter 2:5). The evangelist goes forth to, 'revive the stones out of the heaps of rubbish which are burned...' (Nehemiah 4:2)

Rather than cry; 'Fire in the Hole' the evangelist cries; 'Fire in Hell!'" The evangelist becomes the Gatherer. His grace makes him very effective at Gathering people and finances to reach those who are lost. Many mega-ministries are usually headed by an individual with an evangelist grace upon them.

The Hebrew word that carries the idea of the evangelist is: BASAR. Basar means: to be fresh, to announce (glad news), shew forth (bear, bring, carry, preach, good, tell good), tidings. This Hebrew word speaks of a messenger who preaches, publishes, brings, bears, and carries good tidings.

The Greek has three words that is relative to the ministry of the evangelist. All three words have the same root word. The first word is: <u>EUAGGELIZO</u> which means; 'to announce good news or glad tidings.' This is a description of the evangelist

MINISTRY. The second word is: <u>EUAGGELION</u> which means; 'the gospel or a good message.' This is a description of the *MESSAGE* brought by the evangelist. The third word is: <u>EUGGELISTES</u> which means; 'a preacher or a messenger of good news. It is taken from EU - well, and ANGELOS - a messenger. It speaks of the *PERSON* who is the evangelist, be it male or female.

The Evangelist is one with a gathering ministry, and is a bearer of a good news message.

Jesus Christ is <u>THE</u> Evangelist. Luke's gospel uses the word; 'euggelizo' ten times. His is the messenger who preached, published, and brought good tidings. Luke 4:18 gives us six things that characterized this part of Jesus' ministry.

They are: Preached Good News

                   Healed the Brokenhearted

                   Deliverance to the Captives

                   Recovery of Sight for the Blind

                   Liberty for the Bruised

                   Proclaim the Acceptable Year of the Lord

This ministry was also given to the Body of Christ. (Ephesians 4:11) The difficulty in understanding this ministry is due to the lack of examples and description in the Bible. Other than Christ, we have one good Bible example.

Phillip is the only one specifically called an Evangelist. (Acts 21:8) He will give us a look at the Pattern. The first time we see Phillip, he is selected as a deacon. In Acts 6: 1-7, it states the qualifications for this position. The following should fit the description of every New Testament Evangelist.

Full of the Holy Spirit

Full of Faith

Wisdom

Good Report

Having the Home in Proper Biblical Order

Part of a Local Church

Servant's Heart

These are the minimal requirements found in the life of Phillip.

Phillip reveals to us the four-fold ministry of the New Testament Evangelist. This four fold ministry is as follows:

First, is the PUBLIC Ministry. In Acts 8: 5 - 25, Phillip proceeds to Samaria, a place that was a ready harvest field. This harvest had been sown by Jesus and the woman at the well described in John's Gospel chapter four. The Evangelist is a great reaper and knows how to get the harvest. His message to those bound in sin is centered around Jesus Christ. (Acts 9: 5, 12)

Second, is a SIGNS and WONDERS Ministry. Signs were promised by Jesus Christ to those who would go into all the world and preach the gospel. Phillip's preaching of the good news resulted in unclean spirits coming out of people. We also see the healing of the lame and palsied. Many heard and saw this tremendous demonstration of the Kingdom of God confronting the Kingdom of Darkness.

In many nations that are dominated by False Religions and New Age Philosophy, miracles are signs to that nation of a greater power. One famous leader said to me, "One miracle can open the door to a whole nation that is steeped in darkness." We need Evangelist who will move in the miraculous.

Third, is a PRIVATE Ministry. Phillip demonstrates great balance in his evangelistic ministry. Some evangelist have a great and powerful presence in a crowd, or behind a pulpit, but a true evangelist is ready to share with a group or one on one. An evangelist must be able to read the situation and share the proper message about Jesus Christ. Phillip's ministry to the Ethiopian eunuch in Acts 8: 26-40, reveals how he was ready to share the good news at any time. He was open to the leading and prompting of the Holy Spirit. He was not intimidated by the eunuch's position or authority. Rather, he recognized that the Holy Spirit had prepared the eunuch by the Word. Phillip senses the moment and uses the Old Testament to preach about the saving power of Jesus. The result was the salvation of the eunuch and probably the seed for the gospel to Africa.

I was flying home from some meetings with a friend of mine. This individual has an evangelist grace. When we got on the plane, he told me that he was going to sit across the row from me. I noticed that a young lady was sitting in the same row as my friend. After we reached our cruising level, the stewardess came and took our beverage orders. This young lady ordered a beer. Upon arrival of the beer, my friend began to talk to this young lady. He found out that she was going to Houston because her father was in the Hospital, dying with cancer. My friend started telling her about Jesus. She listened very intently and before we landed he had led her to Jesus. (She never drank from her beverage, she just held it in her hand the whole time)

The Evangelist sees the opportunity and seizes the moment.

Fourth is an EQUIPPING Ministry. One of the gifts given by Christ to the Church is the Evangelist. The Evangelist should be equipping and challenging the saints toward evangelism. Evangelism is a principle function for every Christian to learn and live. Paul tells Timothy: "But watch thou in all things... do the WORK OF AN EVANGELIST." (II Tim. 4:5) The evangelist has the job of bringing the saints to a place of effective evangelism, helping to equip them to evangelize, and helping to make them what they ought to be in God.

In summary, there are several things that characterize the New Testament Evangelist. The evangelist must recognize the limitations of their own ministry. They are not called to do everything, only their areas of authority and strength. The evangelist must understand the need for discernment of the people around them. Phillip gives no indication of recognizing what controlled Simon the Sorcerer. Because evangelists are people oriented they will attract and use all kinds of people, in order to glean the harvest. The evangelist must be willing to work with the other ministry gifts given to the church. The temptation for every evangelist is to become a solo ministry. Finally, an evangelist can not leave the group of new converts unattended. He must encourage, lead, or start a church for these new believers to attend.

We need to come back to the New Testament pattern of an Evangelist. By embracing, encouraging, and supporting the New Testament Evangelist we will see a gathering of the lost and hurting in this world.

AND HE GAVE SOME AS...PASTORS

The pastoral function is one where there has been much misunderstanding and confusion. The term, "Pastor" has been the most accepted of the five fold gifts. In the contemporary Church, the "Pastor" functions in the role of religious administrator, with an office and a staff of religious workers. This role has come to resemble more of a corporation president who has the oversight of a complex institution and organization. The bulk of his time is spent on budgets, building programs, committee meetings, and attendance drives. He is expected to be an all-around, "one man ministry", relating to every one on every level. Resulting in tremendous break down; mentally, emotionally, morally, and spiritually. Burn out is the number one cause of why the average denominational pastorate last approximately twenty two months. Few ministers today seriously interpret their calling as one who is to give himself to the Word and prayer on behalf of the people. Richard Halverson has said that Christianity began in Palestine as a relationship, moved to Greece and became an idea, went to Rome and became an institution, then came to America and became an enterprise!

God's pattern for the Pastor function is simply one of the five fold functions to equip the saints. All Pastors are not apostles, prophets, evangelists, or teachers. There is a distinct Pastor call, that has its own grace, but relates to the other four grace functions. Jesus did give to the Body of Christ some which are distinctly called; 'PASTOR'.

The word 'Pastor' is used several times in the Old Testament and one time in the New Testament. Many other words were used to describe this function; such as shepherd, keeper, feed, herdsman, etc. The combination of these functions reveals to us that a Pastor is one who feeds, tends or herds the flocks, guiding, and ruling. A Pastor is a shepherd. The shepherds of God's people seem to have had military and political powers. (I Chron. 11: 6, Jer. 2: 8, 25: 34-36, 50: 6) The shepherd was one who nourished the flock and furnished pasturage or food. The Greek root word, 'poia' means, "to protect". The shepherd then is one who has a responsibility to care for and protect the sheep from harm. Thayer says that the shepherd in a spiritual sense is; "he to whose care and control others have committed themselves, and whose precepts they follow." "Shepherding people," writes Klaus Bockmuehl, "means to help them grow; it demands thoughtfulness about 'how to make the other one great' and it implies nothing less than the act of true friendship for the others." The shepherding ministry was 'an abomination' to the Egyptians. (Gen. 46:34) So is the Pastoral ministry today to a GODLESS WORLD.

The Lord Jesus Christ is our Pastor and our Shepherd. He is Jehovah-Raah, (Ps. 23:1) "the Lord is my Shepherd". He demonstrated the true shepherd's heart that was part of God's nature. He came and demonstrated in the flesh the Father's love for the flock. Jesus refers to himself as, 'the GOOD Shepherd, (John 10:10) the GREAT Shepherd, (Heb. 13:20) the CHIEF Shepherd, (I Peter 5:4) and the Shepherd and Bishop of our Souls. (I Peter 2:25) Jesus also calls himself, 'the DOOR' (John 10:9) The Greek word, 'Thuroros', is Door or gate-keeper. In the East the door-keeper sat at the entrance of the pen or courtyard to protect the sheep from wild animals in the night. The only way in or out was over the body of the shepherd. By being both, 'Shepherd' and 'Door', John 10:9-10 states that Jesus gives us three things: salvation, finding pasture, and abundant life. Empowering individuals to experience life to the maximum.

Jesus describes himself as the CHIEF Shepherd also. In the East there was a custom of chief shepherds being over those who had large flocks or establishments. He was responsible for the total flock. Christ is the CHIEF Shepherd, but has many 'under shepherds' to help tend and care for the flock. They are His sheep and entrusts His sheep to the shepherding ministry.

A good Pastor must meet all the qualifications for an ELDER described in I Timothy 3. Specific skills and qualities are needed for effective service. Psalms Twenty Three gives us some other areas that must be developed by the Pastor.

(1)   "I shall not want..."   Trust in God must be demonstrated at all times. Trust reflects a pastors knowledge of God's character and his dependence on Him.

(2)   "He makes me to lie down in green pastures..."   The habit of sheep is to remain in the same pastures. Doing this will create a barren field, as sheep will eat all the way down to the roots. A wise shepherd knows when to lead to different areas and how long to stay in that location. Green pastures are not common in the East. They must be cultivated, this takes time, work, and skill. Green pastures are essential for the maturing and reproducing of sheep. The Pastor also must take the flock to fields of prayer, tithing, fellowship, life in the Spirit, family, etc. While he has led them to one field, while they eat or rest, the Pastor must be preparing the next field.

(3)   "He leadeth me beside still waters..." Sheep are fearful of rushing water. If they were to fall in with their heavy wool coats it could mean instant death. The Pastor must know where the people can drink and how much. Exposing and healing fears is a major responsibility.

(4)   "He restoreth my soul..." Sheep 'nip' away at living plants until they reach the roots. The Pastor must know how to pull down strongholds and put people on the path of doing what is right.

(5)   "I will fear NO evil, for thou art with me..." The eastern shepherd names all of his sheep. This is similar to us naming our dogs, cats, or birds. He eats, talks, sleeps, walks, and cares for the sheep. The Pastor must know his people, and allow them to know him.

He must identify with them, sit with them, and let them know he is a sheep also.

(6)   "Thy rod and thy staff they comfort me..."   Sheep will wander away from the protection of the shepherd. When this happens their thick coats can get caught in the underbrush, causing them to be held captive till they die. They also become exposed to their predators or fall into crevices, eating wrong things, etc. If one of the sheep continually goes astray, the shepherd will break one of the legs and then nurse the sheep back to life. The Pastor must become skillful with the Rod. The rod is a symbol of Authority. It was used primarily to drive enemies away. When people become ensnared by the Devil, the Pastor must know how to exercise authority against him. The Staff was to snatch the animal that had fallen off a cliff or into a crevice. It represents an instrument of guidance. The Pastor must know how to give Godly counsel for those who are seeking God's will. They also must be able to warn and snatch those who have fallen.

(7)   "Thou preparest a table before me in the presence of mine enemies, thou anointest my head will oil..."   Sheep are defenseless. They have no way of protecting themselves. They cannot kick, bite, or hide. Since sheep have no built-in defense system, they have many who prey upon them. Sheep also attract many bugs, parasites and are often scratched or bitten. The shepherd will pour a specially prepared mixture of oil, tar, and herbs over the head of the sheep. The Pastor must know how to bring people to the table of the Lord. Upon coming to that table there will be healing, deliverance, and fresh anointing.

In summary, the Pastor's role is best described by C. W. Fleming in his book, <u>"He Leadeth Me."</u> He gives several thoughts about the shepherd's equipment.

Fleece sheepskin coat for warmth for himself and lambkins   (Jer. 43:13)

A Wallet for carrying food (I Sam. 17:40)

A sling and staff for beastly enemy attacks (Ps 23:4)
An oil bottle, protection against vipers and parasites on the sheep

A reed flute for music, song, that the sheep enjoy

A lamp for his feet in the darkness of the night

We continue some more thoughts on this subject in future editions. Until then let us pray for the pastoral function.

Now that we have looked at the qualifications of the Pastor grace, it is now time to examine some of his responsibilities. The Pastor grace leans more toward mercy and compassion than any of the five-fold functional gifts. Caring and counseling are a major focus of his day to day ministry. Because of this nature, this gift battles much depression, doubt, and discouragement. One man said, "We never get down about something we DO NOT love." This is very true, especially when the Pastoral grace is trying to move a group of people to a place in God.

One day a friend met his pastor working at the local funeral home. Surprised, the man asked, "What are you doing here?" The pastor replied, " I work here!" "Don't we pay you enough?" asked the friend. "Oh yes," said the pastor, "but when I straighten a person out here, he stays straight!!"

God gave Adam two commands in the garden. First, 'Dress It' Second, 'Keep It' <u>Dress it</u> means: to work, till, to make weary, fatigued, and worship. <u>Keep it</u> means: to hedge around, to guard, to watch, to keep safe from outside intruders, and to preserve.

This is very similar to the responsibility of the Pastoral grace. He has been placed in a local church to work and till the ground. This is done through much labor. Our garden is the place where God has put us to work. When we fulfill that responsibility, it then becomes an act of worship unto God. (Romans 12:1-2 NAS) When worship is expressed, demonic activity will come to pervert that relationship. The pastor is to keep the local church from this demonic activity. Because of the Fall, Satan tries to move us to be independent of authority. The pastor is the gatekeeper and watcher who guards the entrance into the sheepfold.

The scriptures reveal our need for leadership at this entrance.

Let me list a few:

Gen 4:7	". . .sin lieth at the door".
Gen 18:1-10	Place of meeting God.
Ex 33:8-10	Place of worship.
II Kgs 7:3-11	Place of rulership

Hosea 2:4   Place to receive hope

Acts 14:27   Opens the door of Faith

Col 4:3   Utterance of the gospel

James 5:29   Place of Judging

A pastor will watch for fruitfulness and increase. He must also be alert to all forms of attack. The entrance is a key area of responsibility.

The pastor is also responsible for leading the people of God. He will not drive the sheep or overdrive them. Gen 33:10-18 gives a beautiful picture of how the shepherd led the flock. This is the account of Jacob leading his flock as he went back to his home country. The following list describes Jacob's attitude and responsibility toward his flock.

* Kind of People he was leading---. . . .the children. . .

The pastor realizes that all of his flock are God's children. Growth is slow and deliberate.

* Condition of the People---. . .tender. . . Prov 27:23 states, "Be thou diligent to know the state of they flocks, and look well to thy herds."

State=condition. Look well=observation. The flocks and herds had young with them. The pastor must be sensitive to the growth and maturing process of the church.

* Know what the flock can and cannot handle---". . . if man should overdrive them, one day ALL the flock will die. . ."

It is the pastor's responsibility to know when its time to bring change. How much financial burden they can handle? If they are ready for leadership and what kind. Help people find their proper place and gifting. When people lack these things, notice ALL people begin to die.

* Makes the decision to lead, not someone else---". . . let my lord (Esau), pass over before his servant. . ."

The pastor's grace keeps the people focused on the vision of the house. He should not be concerned or competitive with what another group is doing. The pastor must have a style that is his own. Notice, Jacob led "softly". Don't try to mimic what someone else is doing. What works for another group, may not be God's way for you.

* Focus on things that have longevity " . . be able to endure. ."

The pastor's responsibility is to keep the world system out; therefore, we do not need fleshly methods to accomplish God's purpose. Gifting without character results in carnality. What we build with our gifts, we will eventually destroy with our lack of Godly character.

The pastoral function is so vital. It states in verse 18, "And Jacob came to Shalom. . ." The results of the pastoral grace is peace in our life, family, and church. Embrace this gift and receive the peace that passes all understanding. The command to the pastoral grace is to "WATCH". (Matt 13:32-37)

The following article by *Mary M. Darrell* entitled, <u>"What is a Pastor"</u>, gives a view of a person in the congregation and how they view the pastor. Her insight lays the ground work for some cautions I want to share with the local pastors. She writes.

"This sheep has been puzzled by the many strange "shepherding" ideas that seem to abound throughout the "pastures" of the land. So I consulted a copy of the

Shepherding Manual and it seemed that the Good Shepherd had the following concepts in mind concerning what a pastor should be.

A Pastor is a Shepherd. He is the expression of Jehovah Rohi - - Jehovah, my Shepherd - - to the flocks of God.

A Pastor, first and foremost, loves his sheep. His is not a part-time love, nor is it conditional. It is not based on outward appearances. His love is for the weak and for the strong alike. His sheep have priority over any outside the flock.

A Pastor would, and does, give his life for his flock. He positions himself between his flock and the wolves, and his sling drives away the enemy. He looks to the good of the whole flock and wields his rod of correction when necessary. He rules the flock from the position of a servant and does not lord it over them. When the sheep have fallen or been wounded, He is there to pour in the oil and bind up their wounds.

A pastor delights in the growth and maturity of his flock. He is not in competition with them but rather rejoices when they move out in gifts and ministry. He takes special pleasure over those who bring forth lambs and over those who nurture their young.

A Pastor is on his knees daily before his Master Shepherd. He does not ask for silver-tongued oratory nor to be lifted up among his fellow-shepherds. He does not ask for the biggest flock around, nor for woollier sheep, nor for bigger shears. He asks for direction to the pastures of the Master Shepherd's choosing. He desires for the mind of his Master in all matters - - and especially to be like Him in His nature.

A Pastor has vision. He envisions his sheep healthy and growing. He envisions each one's capabilities, even though at first the talents may seem to be hidden. He envisions enlargement of the flock through the reproduction of the sheep. He envisions his flock increasing and spreading over the hillsides of the land. He also envisions the growth and well-being of all the flocks of God.

So, you see, this sheep cares little about some of those other shepherding ideas. I mean, how important is it if a Shepherd works out three times a week at the local gym -

- or if he has the sharpest wardrobe in six counties.

or if he hobnobs with the Best Pastors and Name-Brand Evangelists.

or if his "prosperity message" has brought him a Mercedes and three Cadillacs.

or if he is listed among "The Ten most . . . . ."?

This sheep looks for the love and tender-kindness of a True Shepherd.

This sheep appreciates the green pastures for a hungry heart as well as the rod of correction, for it brings security.

This sheep gladly receives the words of the Master Shepherd brought by a True Undershepherd.

This sheep will not rebel at the authority of a Shepherd who rules with the basin and towel of a servant.

This sheep will follow such a Shepherd in his vision, and will go in and out of the sheepfold with rejoicing."

What do you think?

Pastors are ministries who have been ordained by God to nurture and care for the local church. God requires accountability from ALL ministries which will appear before the Lord to give an account of their responsibilities. These responsibilities will be tested by fire as we stand before Him. (I Cor. 3: 10-15) *Acts 20: 28* states, "Take heed (beware, be cautious) therefore unto yourselves, and to the flock, over the which the Holy Ghost hath made YOU overseers..." God gives the local pastor a warning in order to protect His people. There are several cautions that God gives to those who pastor His flock.

First, is the BUSY SCHEDULE syndrome.

Leadership today is full of activity, events, conferences, and busyness. One could attend an event or conference every day of the week. Many times these serve as substitutes for quality time with God. C. Peter Wagner writes in his book, _Prayer Shield_, out of 572 American pastors interviewed, the following data came forth.

57% pray less than 20 minutes a day

34% pray between 20 minutes and one hour

9% pray one hour or more per day

The average prayer time was 22 minutes daily

The fruit of busy schedules is _IMAGE BUILDING_. Image building leaders find their identity more in performance and appearance than in a Christ-centered ministry. When we neglect quality time with the head of the church we leave the door open for continual demonic attacks. The attack is not only on leaders, but the entire church.

Here are some symptoms that surface when the pastor neglects this quality time.

- Much work, but little progress toward the vision
- Quick growth for a season, followed by devastating conflict
- Apparent progress, but quickly fades away
- Church maintains, but has little power

We must be aware of Satan's desire to misplace priorities and cause us to get caught up in the spirit of the hour.

Secondly, is the GO FOR THE GOLD syndrome.

Glen Buck states, "If your capacity to acquire has outstripped your capacity to enjoy, you are on your way to the scrap-heap." Because we live in a Global world economy, the greatest battle today is with mammon. Much of the world is not controlled by local or national governments, but by the decisions of the Federal Reserve Bank. Whenever its chairperson speaks the stocks rise or fall several points on any given day. In _John 10_, Jesus is explaining the different kinds of shepherds (pastors). Three out of the five had to do with money. He warned of thieves, robbers, and hirelings. A thief is one who usually likes to operate under the cover of darkness and steals from you when you are away. A robber is one who steals by force, day or night. The hireling is one who is just paid to do a job. When trouble begins to arise, he begins looking for the next assignment. When revival comes, abundance is released to the church. The greatest temptation in revival is responsible discretion of financial management. How do we stay balanced in this area? The answer is rather easy. "What you teach others about financial responsibility, give your instruction power by doing the same."

Thirdly, is the EL JEFE syndrome.

El Jefe is the Spanish phrase for 'THE BOSS'. Many people look at the pastorate as an opportunity to be in charge, the boss, in control, etc. This person is always looking for someone to serve them. El Jefe's characteristics are:

- They operate from a false basis of authority
- They lack integrity
- Their spirituality is on the outside
- Spiritual is based on performance, and image they project
- They require recognition of people, calling it RESPECT
- They are the source of all knowledge, direction, authority, and life

Being a pastor is a position of authority. That authority comes from humble servanthood. I am most like Jesus when I am serving. What we seek in rewards, we must demonstrate in service for others.

Fourthly, the CATTLE DRIVING syndrome

Before they would begin the long cattle drives from south Texas to the stockyards of Kansas, they would make sure the cattle were fat and healthy. This took time and only the healthy were selected. The rancher understood that during the long journey north, water would be scarce and feeding minimal, resulting in the loss of weight. This loss was costly, as he received compensation based on the weight of the cattle. Pastors receive much revelation, insight and lifestyle in order to feed and lead the people. When a pastor receives new insight he wants others to walk in it immediately. The people do not have the capacity to receive or comprehend truth as easily and quickly as the pastor. Thus, the pastor must be patient. He must know the pace and maturity of the whole congregation. New insights must be introduced methodically and slowly in order for the whole congregation to move forward.

If we will heed some of these warnings, lives will be enriched, congregations made whole and the pastoral function rewarding.

AND HE GAVE SOME AS...TEACHERS

The primary purpose of education in biblical times was to train the whole person for lifelong, obedient service in the knowledge of God. (Pr. 1:7; Eccl. 12:13) The aim of learning was holiness in living - to be set apart unto God in every dimension of life. Everything God does, He does based on principles. Our lives must be ordered based on these principles. It is interesting that every fresh move of God did not take hold until the truth around which the move was built, was expounded from the Scriptures.

Matthew 28:20 states, "...teaching them to observe all things whatsoever I commanded you." In order to disciple and change nations the work of teaching must be paramount. In order to meet this challenge God has given TEACHERS to the Body of Christ. The ministry of the teacher is a very important ministry if babes are to grow up into Him in all things.

Jesus is called: Master, Rabbi, and Teacher. During New Testament times the land had many teachers and their followers. Jesus was one such teacher in the scribal tradition (Mt. 13:52). The Gospels refer to Jesus as *didaskalos,* 'teacher,' forty-one times and as 'rabbi' sixteen times. Like a scribe, he teaches in synagogues (Mk. 1:21), sits to teach (Lk 5:3), and expounds Scripture (Lk. 4: 16-21). In Jesus' day the word *rabbi* was a popular term of honor meaning "my master" or "my great one". Jesus fulfilled both of these titles to those who followed Him. His style and material was essential for the young disciples to learn. He taught everywhere He went; in the homes, synagogues, streets, and temple. He used a mixture of preaching, teaching, and healing. He taught with anointing and authority. What made His teaching so successful was the fact that He only taught what the Father had given to Him.

The definition for Teacher is derived from several different words, both in Hebrew and Greek. The Hebrew words are:

> *Yarah* (SC 3384) =   'to flow as water, to rain; fig, to point out (as if by aiming the finger), to teach.

> *Lamad* (SC 3925) =   'to goad, i.e., [by implication] to teach (the rod being an Oriental incentive).

Together these words show that a Teacher is one who points out by the finger, directs, informs, instructs, shoots with an archer, and shows, by teaching the ways of the Lord. His teaching is to flow like water, and let it come down like rain. He is the one who is skilful in instruction and causes others to learn. His teaching is like a goad, a rod, that causes the people of God to walk in the ways of the Lord.

The New Testament Greek word that is used in regards to the teaching ministry is the word, *"didasko"*. The root meaning of this word simply means, 'to instruct'. A teacher is one who instructs, and by his teaching causes others to learn. It involves exposition, explanation, and instruction of doctrine to others.

The Old Testament had no system or network of formal schooling, and professional schooling was not readily available to the masses. The home was the main center for learning. Both parents shared the responsibility of training the children. The main responsibility was on the father for instruction of the children. Others were important influences on the training of the young. They were the: PRIESTS, PROPHETS, and WISE MEN (Jer. 18:18)

PRIESTS were the custodians and proclaimers of the law. Deut. 17:11 "...act according to the law they (the priests) teach you..."

PROPHETS were the leaders of righteousness and social justice. They were constantly reminding the people to return to the teachings of the law.

WISE MEN imparted knowledge to the people. (Eccl. 12:9) They reflected on perplexing issues of life and made prudent observations on them. Their most common function was to give wisdom or counsel to people needing practical advice for living.

The New Testament Teacher is summed up in the definition of the term. The Teacher should be able to take the truth of God's word, both in the Old and New Testament, and expound with clarity and inspiration. Because the Teacher appeals more to the LOGIC of the people, he needs to depend more on the Holy Spirit's unction and insight. (Eph. 1: 17-18)

The fivefold ministries may be grouped (without being limited to such) into two groups:

INSPIRATIONAL	LOGICAL
Quickening	Illumination
Appeal to the Emotions	Appeals to the Intellect
Preaching	Teaching

Apostle

Prophets	Pastors
Evangelists	Teachers

These may involve preaching and teaching and overlap into both areas, both inspirational and logical.

The Teacher, by reason of his nature, appeals more to the understanding, reason, intelligence, and logic than to the emotions. He is especially systematic, following the rules of logic. His will be a ministry of the Spirit and the Word. He will compare "spiritual things with spiritual".

The believer needs to receive the Teacher in order to receive the benefits of his labors in the Word. The benefits are numerous as we embrace this gift. A few of these benefits are:

Edification - much teaching today is composed of jokes, psychology, and social concerns. Good teaching has solid content and substance. The material is presented in such a way that uses the above forms, but is based on biblical principles, resulting in the learner being edified and built up.

Explaining Ideas - the Hebrew word "bin" means; 'to distinguish, separate.' This word is the idea of separating, evaluating, or distinguishing one thing from another, in the sense of taking an idea or argument apart. The Teacher has the ability to separate, explain issues, and to solve problems.

Piercing the Heart - Deut 6:7 states, "...and thou shalt teach them diligently..." This phrase also means to sharpen, whet, pierce, or prick. The Teacher should present God's word in a way that will sharpen and prick the hearts of the learner.

Guidance - like an archer, a teacher has something to shoot out or project, guiding it toward a specific target. He has an aim and a goal. Even though, the Teacher is not the Holy Spirit, his teaching can be a confirmation and clarification of what the Holy Spirit has spoken.

Training & Discipline - The Teacher has not taught properly unless the student has learned. This requires both information and practical application. The Teacher demonstrates a disciplined life of the truths he is attempting to impart. In the Egyptian language, the word '*sebayet*' is translated either 'to teach' or 'punishment'. In pictographic Egyptian language, part of the word 'to teach' is the picture of a man hitting with a stick. While the Teacher does not use hitting as a method of training, discipline is essential to all learning.

The Teacher is another valuable ministry. By embracing this gift our grounding in the word of God will be greatly strengthened.

TAKE UP YOUR TOWEL

BY DAVID WILKERSON

In a famous passage in John 13, Jesus took a towel and a basin and washed the feet of His disciples. He told them:

"If I then, your Lord and Master, have washed your feet; ye also ought to wash one another's feet" (John 13:14).

Some devout Christians take this verse literally. They have made it their custom to have "foot washing" services. This is commendable - yet, if it remains only a ritual, the true meaning of foot washing has been lost.

After Jesus washed the disciples' feet, He put His garment back on, sat down and asked them, "Do you know what I've just done to you?" In other words: "Do you understand the spiritual significance of foot washing?"

I believe the Lord's question is for us today as well. Indeed, something very powerful and profound was taking place; Christ was teaching His church one of its most important lessons. Yet, do we understand the depths of what Jesus did in washing the disciples' feet?

Jesus was not instituting an ordinance to be carried on throughout the church ages, such as communion or water baptism. If that were so, He would have instituted it at the beginning of the disciples' training. And Hewould have submitted to a foot washing Himself, as He had done with water baptism.

I pored over my Bible commentaries to see what the church fathers have said about this scene. Almost without exception, they wrote that its significance is in Jesus' example of humility. He took the lowly place to show us how to be humble. Yet I believe this interpretation misses the meaning of the passage entirely. After all, Jesus had already set an example of humility by taking on human form - by laying aside His glory and coming to earth as a servant.

No - this passage says so much more than that! I believe Jesus was giving us an example of the kind of physical manifestation He desires most - that of "taking up the towel"!

Today, when we speak of manifestations, we think of people in church meetings falling to the ground. To many, that kind of manifestation seems strange. Yet, as you study the Word of God, you learn that Jesus talked a lot about unusual physical manifestations.

Jesus didn't talk about falling to the ground. But He did speak of falling into the ground and dying - to bear fruit! He spoke of the manifestation of taking up a cross - of cutting off an offending hand, plucking out an offensive eye, going an extra mile.

Yet one of the most unusual of all the manifestations Christ talked about is His call to take up the towel. Throughout my years in ministry, many people have asked, "Why don't we wash each other's feet in church, as Jesus told us to? He said, 'If I do it, you should do it, too.'"

I usually answered, "What Jesus is talking about is primarily a spiritual thing, and not just physical." Yet even as I said this, I had no concept of the spiritual meaning of foot washing.

We gloss over certain truths in the Bible because we don't understand their meaning - and for years we miss the power of these passages. For example, Scripture tells us:

"...by love serve one another" (Galatians 5:13).

And: "(Submit) yourselves one to another in the fear of God" (Ephesians 5:21).

How many of us really know what it means to serve one another in love? And how are we supposed to submit to one another in the fear of God? It's easy enough to understand how a wife is to submit to the spiritual authority of a godly husband. And the same is true for children submitting to godly parents. But in what practical ways do we serve and submit to one another in the house of God?

I believe that if we understand what Jesus did in washing His disciples' feet, we will understand these concepts of service and submission. You see, serving one another in love and submitting to one another in godly fear mean much more than taking orders from or being accountable to a higher authority. Rather, these glorious truths are unlocked only in the context of "taking up the towel."

While I was in prayer recently, the Holy Spirit gave me three words to open my understanding about this matter of taking up the towel. The three words are dirt, comfort and unity. Hopefully, as we examine these words, the Holy Ghost will unlock to us His truth:

1. Let Us Begin With the Matter of Dirt Clinging to A Christian Brother or Sister!

The disciples were twelve men beloved of God - precious in His eyes, full of love for His Son, pure-hearted, in full communion with Jesus. Yet they had dirt on their feet!

Jesus, in essence, was saying to these men, "Your hearts and hands are clean, but your feet are not. They've gotten dirty in your daily walk with Me. You don't need your whole body to be washed - only your feet."

The dirt Jesus mentions here has nothing to do with natural dirt. It's all about sin - our faults and failures, our giving in to temptations. And no matter how dusty and dirty the roads were in ancient Jerusalem, no age was ever as filthy as ours!

I wonder how many people reading this message right now have some dirt clinging to them. Perhaps this past week you fell into a temptation or failed God in some way. It's not that you've turned your back on the Lord. On the contrary - you love the Savior more passionately than ever. But you fell, and now you're grieving - because your feet are dirty!

Scripture tells us:

"Brethren, if a man be overtaken in a fault, ye which are spiritual, restore such an one in the spirit of meekness; considering thyself, lest thou also be tempted" (Galatians 6:1).

The Greek word for fault here means "a fall, a sin, a transgression." We are to restore every Christian who falls into sin, if there is a repentant heart.

And foot washing, in its deepest spiritual meaning, has to do with our attitude about the dirt we see on our brother or sister. So, I ask you:

What do you do when you're face to face with someone who has fallen into a sin or transgression?

What you do about the dirt on your brother or sister has everything to do with the ministry Jesus describes as "taking up the towel." It has everything to do with how you serve others in love and submit to others in the fear of God.

Let me say very clearly: Christians can be very cruel! In fact, believers often are more vicious and destructive than the wicked in the streets. And Jesus knew that. He knew how we react to the sight of dirt on someone else - how we put on a holier-than-thou attitude, judging, gossiping and slandering. Indeed, carnal Christians delight in seeing dirt on others. But their spreading of the dirt is the dirtiest sin of all!

In recent weeks, I've been trying to encourage a young pastor who resigned from his church after confessing a moral transgression. This dear man loves the Lord. He has a heart for people and for God's Word. But his feet got dirty! Yet he is totally repentant.

As soon as I heard about his fall and resignation, the Holy Spirit instructed me to get in touch with him immediately. I knew this young pastor was still a good man. He hadn't suddenly become wicked. His heart wasn't hardened over his sin. Yet his best friends forsook him. Those who claimed to love him most now ignored him, as if he had an infectious disease. To top it off, his denominational leaders demanded he make a video of his confession - giving every vivid detail of his transgression.

I called this dear brother - and I took a towel with me. I left a message on his answering machine, saying: "Brother, I want you to know I love you. God isn't finished with you. If you have a repentant heart, the Lord will restore you. And I'm going to stand with you!"

Beloved, taking up a towel is an attitude, a commitment. It means doing all within our power to cleanse the dirt off our brother's feet. It says, "I'm committed to helping you clean off the dirt - to restore your reputation, your family - to do everything to keep you alive in Christ!"

A friend of this pastor later called me. He said, "David, you will never know what your phone call meant to my friend - how blessed, encouraged and comforted he was. No one else has reached out to him. Your words gave him new hope."

Scripture clearly states that whenever a brother or sister has been overtaken in a sin, we must restore that person - serving him in love, submitting to him in the fear of God. Yet, you may ask, how are we to do this?

We are to take up the towel of God's mercy and go to that hurting one. In the special love of Jesus, we are to submit all of our human inclinations to ignore him, judge him, expose him, lecture him and find fault with him - and, instead, we are to commit to being his friend. We are to help wash away his sins by sharing the correcting, healing, washing, comforting Word of God.

This is not overlooking or winking at sin. It is not calling evil good. We're talking about fallen saints who have repentant hearts yet are without hope. They know they have grieved the Lord - and they live with fear, guilt, rejection.

It's a different matter entirely with those who have been warned two or three times yet persist in their sin. The Bible says we are to sharply rebuke such believers in public so that others may fear God. Often they must be disfellowshiped for a season, until they demonstrate godly sorrow.

But those who acknowledge their sin - who confess it and forsake it - are in need of someone to bring the towel of mercy, to bring them cleansing and healing.

A few years ago, an associate pastor of a very large church called me in tears. He told me, "Brother David, I can't keep my head up, I'm so broken."

He described to me the pain he experienced when his teenage daughter became pregnant outside of marriage. The senior pastor of the church demanded that this associate go before the congregation and tell them what his daughter had done.

This dear man did just that - and it devastated his daughter. It broke the family's heart. But the congregation wallowed in all the details of the poor teenage girl's sin.

Then, a year later, the senior pastor's teenage daughter became pregnant. But this time, the senior pastor did everything in his power to cover it up.

God, have mercy on us - because we destroy people who get dirt on their feet! When will we ever learn to take up the towel of mercy - to commit ourselves to cleansing and restoring, rather than throwing dirt into the wind and destroying precious souls?

2. Those Who Take Up the Towel Are the True Comforters Whom the Holy Ghost Uses!

Do you know what it's like to be barefoot and have to walk through mud? The dirt that cakes on your feet can be truly miserable. You feel much better when your feet are washed and clean.

When Jesus washed the dirt from His disciples' feet, they were comforted. But, spiritually speaking, Jesus was teaching the comfort of transgressions removed!

In 1 Corinthians 5, we read of a man in the church who fell into the terrible sin of incest. Evidently the man was unrepentant, and Paul directed the church to turn him over to Satan for the destruction of his flesh (that is, to the saving of his spirit). Paul was not saying the man was lost and going to hell. No - he only wanted him isolated from fellowship and given over to Satan's devices, so he would come to his wits' end and be driven to repentance.

Later, in 2 Corinthians 2, Paul found out the same man had become repentant and that the church had forgiven him. Satan had brought him to despair, and the lust in his flesh had been destroyed. The man had come back repentant. And now Paul wrote to the Corinthians:

"...ye ought rather to forgive him, lest perhaps such a one should be swallowed up with overmuch sorrow. Wherefore I beseech you that ye would confirm your love toward him" (2 Corinthians 2:7-8).

Paul knew this man was absolutely overwhelmed with grief and sorrow. Those in the church had seen his brokenness and humility, and they were overcome with a spirit of mercy. They encouraged him, were tenderhearted toward him and washed his feet. Now he was clean - and he was being restored to the body of Jesus Christ. What a wonderful picture!

There are many Christians today who are in the same condition as this man, after being overtaken by a sin. They say to themselves, "I have reproached my Savior. I've brought shame to His name!" Yet what they experience is nothing like what 2 Corinthians describes.

I want to show you a passage from a book I received not long ago. It was written by the daughter of a pastor who was overtaken by a sin several years ago. And for all those years the family has endured a nightmarish hell. She writes:

"...(The press) followed us to our homes. We got phone calls from famous gossip tabloids offering large sums of money for a story. We'd finally succeed in getting Dad out of the house and into a restaurant, only to find ourselves the subject of people's conversations. It was horrible.

"But Reverend _______ was never ashamed to identify with us. Dad would literally sit by the phone awaiting this man's call. He was overcome with guilt and shame.... Dad had sunken into deep depression.... People to whom he gave so much of himself were the ones who turned against him so harshly.

"New rumors were spread daily. Ministers wrote to one another, spreading those rumors.... Only a select few proved true by showing Christian love and restoration, by calling us and remembering us in their prayers."

I know the man this daughter is describing. He is a dedicated man of God, a good father and a caring pastor. His heart is still passionately in love with Jesus. In fact, he has been restored and is pastoring a growing church.

Yet, can you imagine how he has felt all these years? Everyone he'd ministered to for years turned against him - including those he'd won to Christ! He was devastated, overwhelmed with sorrow. At one point his daughter suggested to her husband that they take the gun out of the man's house, fearing that in his depression he might be overcome by thoughts of suicide.

This lonely, despairing man waited by the phone for a call from his faithful pastor friend. The loving, compassionate minister was the only one willing to bring a towel to his friend - a little comfort, a word of encouragement, a brief moment of laughter.

Can you blame the fallen, dejected pastor for wanting just a little relief from the long years of pain inflicted by God's people and other ministers?

3.	The World Outside the Church Has Become Demonized With the Spirit Of Hate -Character Assassination, Slander, Destruction of Reputations And Families

No sooner does a politician announce he's running for office than the press turns into a pack of vultures, digging into his past life just to find some dirt. And when they find it, they plaster it across the headlines, for all of America to wallow in.

America has gone crazy with slander! TV is rife with talk shows featuring gossip, exposure, mockery. The wicked get their thrills from destroying people, families, good reputations. And the more lurid the dirt, the more the people love it.

But this kind of thing has no place in God's house. The church ought to be different. It ought to be a house of cleansing!

The Gentiles in Ephesus honored God's people by calling them "Christians, "meaning, "kindhearted." They had seen how kindhearted these believers were toward others.

"And be ye kind one to another, tenderhearted, forgiving one another, even as God for Christ's sake hath forgiven you" (Ephesians 4:32).

If you want to be kindhearted - to take up the towel to restore a brother or sister - you don't need to know the details of how that person got dirty. Jesus did not ask His disciples, "How did you get such dirty feet?" He wanted only to accomplish their cleansings - to get the dirt off of them. His love for them was unconditional.

Likewise, those who walk in the fullness of Jesus Christ must also have this attitude of love toward those with dirty feet. We aren't to ask for details. Instead, we're to say, "Let's do something about the dirt!"

But too often, this isn't the case. Many Christians want to delve into all the gory details. They come to a believer who has dirty feet, saying, "I want to wash your feet. But, tell me - what happened? How'd you get so dirty?"

Then, at some point in the story of failure, the curious comforter realizes, "Oh, my - this is worse than I thought. I can't get involved in this. I can't handle it." And after two minutes of details, he comes to the end of his puny human mercy. He judges the person as too evil, beyond help - and chooses to ignore him. He drops his towel and goes his way.

Beloved, you can't wash feet in a judge's robes! You have to take off your self-righteous garments - your holier-than-thou attitude - before you can do any cleansing. Like Jesus, you must lay aside your outer garment and gird yourself with love. Off with all self-righteousness - all pride, all thoughts that you could never stoop so low! You must have an attitude that says, "I don't care what you did. If you're repentant and want to hear God's Word, I'll be kind and tenderhearted to you!"

Yet, you ask, what if the dirty person before you is a Judas - someone who has betrayed you? My answer to you is, Judas was in that room with the other disciples, and Jesus washed his feet too. Christ stooped to cleanse Judas' dirt, even though Satan had already put betrayal in his heart.

Indeed, modern-day Judases can be saved because of the Cross. Often we think of certain sinners, such as homosexuals or lesbians, as being hopelessly hooked. We think they can never be delivered. Yet Paul says of them:

"Know ye not that the unrighteous shall not inherit the kingdom of God? Be not deceived: neither fornicators, nor idolaters, nor adulterers, nor effeminate, nor abusers of themselves with mankind [homosexuals], nor thieves, nor covetous, nor drunkards, nor revilers, nor extortioners, shall inherit the kingdom of God.

"And such were some of you: but ye are washed, but ye are sanctified, but ye are justified in the name of the Lord Jesus, and by the Spirit of our God" (1 Corinthians 6:9-11).

Such were some of us - but we had our feet washed by Jesus! I ask you - if Jesus is willing to justify all sinners, why aren't we willing to wash those sinners' feet?

Paul says we are to be gentle and patient with all people:

"And the servant of the Lord must not strive; but be gentle unto all men, apt to teach, patient, in meekness instructing those that oppose themselves; if God peradventure will give them repentance to the acknowledging of the truth; and that they may recover themselves out of the snare of the devil, who are taken captive by him at his will"

(2 Timothy 2:24-26).

Paul is saying, "You've got to be tenderhearted with everyone, to be willing to wash their feet. God may have mercy on them yet - and deliver them from their sin!"

Our church has spent almost thirty weeks now praying for revival in New York City. Yet, it doesn't matter how much a church prays; God will not plant new believers there if they're going to have to struggle amid a bunch of judging, self-centered Christians.

You see, every new believer is going to get his feet dirty before he becomes established in the faith. And he needs people who are willing to go to him quickly to wash his feet and restore him. True revival reflects this spirit of kindness - a spirit that's willing to take up the towel to cleanse and restore dirty believers!

4.   Finally, We Come to the Word Unity!

I believe when Jesus washed the disciples' feet, He was teaching a profound lesson on how to obtain unity of fellowship in the body of Christ.

As Jesus approached Peter to wash his feet, the disciple drew back. "...Peter saith unto him, Lord, dost thou wash my feet?" (John 13:6). Peter asked in astonishment, "Lord, You aren't going to wash my feet, are You? Never, never!" Jesus answered, "...If

I wash thee not, thou hast no part with me" (verse 8).

Jesus was saying, in essence, "Peter, if I wash your feet, we have precious grounds for fellowship, a basis for true unity." Likewise, no pastor can bring unity into a church simply by implementing programs or even by his fiery preaching. No - unity comes from taking up a towel!

After Jesus washed His disciples' feet, He asked them, "Do you understand what I have done to you?" If they had understood the spiritual significance of what He had just done - taking away the stain and guilt of their sin - it would have produced in them gratitude.

I ask you: What did Jesus do to you when He cleansed you? He wiped away all your fault and guilt - He cleansed the last remnants of sin - and you were made clean, whole. He put gratitude, thankfulness, joy in your soul. He filled you with such love for Him that you would follow Him anywhere and do anything for Him. All you wanted was communion with Him, because of what He did for you.

Beloved, that is the secret of unity! When you take up the towel of mercy for a hurting, fallen brother, you encourage him by embracing him in his hurt - by submitting in godly fear, washing away his feelings of worthlessness, anguish and despair, and by loving and caring for him.

Yet, what have you done to that person by washing his feet? You have constructed a firm foundation for true unity and glorious fellowship. You are one by your common experience - that is, by being washed by the water of the Word!

Talk about gratitude - that Christian will be your friend for life! He will defend you, love you, do anything for you. He'll say to you, "You stood with me in my hard times. And now I'll never let anyone do anything to you!"

Can you imagine a church filled with such caring people - who refuse to hear a single word about another's dirt; who hurt when another hurts; who rally around every despairing, fault-ridden brother or sister with a word of love and hope? That is why we moved our ministry to New York City - to raise up a holy, godly remnant who would make up a strong, unified base of comforters - people who carry a towel in their hands!

You may ask, "But how do I find people whose feet need washing?" My answer to you is, "The same way you found them when you gossiped about them!"

Now, whenever you hear anything negative about someone, merely ask, "Who are you talking about? Name only, please!" Then go to that hurting person quickly with your mercy towel - and start washing his feet! Tell the fallen one, "I care about you. And I want to pray for you - but I don't need to know any details. I just want you to know I still love you - and I'm going to stand with you!"

This message is for me as much as for anyone else. I have just recently come into this convicting knowledge of what foot washing is truly about. And, by God's grace, I'll take up the towel of mercy along with others and seek out those hurting ones whose feet need cleansing from dirt.

Jesus said, "If I then, as your Lord and Master, have washed your feet; ye also ought to wash one another's feet.... If ye know these things, happy are ye if ye do them" (John 13:14, 17).

Now that we "know these things," as Jesus said, we can do them. I ask you: Are you willing to do them? Are you ready to take up your towel in love?

Hallelujah!

ABOUT THE AUTHOR

Dr Terry L . Thompson is an internationally known conference speaker, lecturer, and trainer. Terry and Becky, founded and established Global Leadership Network in Montgomery, Texas; a metropolitan suburb of the Greater Houston area.

Terry was born in Malvern, Iowa; a small farming town in the southwest corner of the state. It was in this area that he was first exposed to the love and biblical principles of God's word. Then in his early teen years the family moved to Texas. After serving a tour of duty in Vietnam, Terry returned to pursue his desire to be a professional basketball coach. He enrolled at Southwestern Assembly of God University, where he played and set several school records in basketball. The one record that means the most was when he knelt in a basketball dressing room and invited Jesus Christ into his life. During the campus spring revival, Terry gave his life for full time ministry.

In the summer of 1972, Terry and Becky were married. They now have two sons; Shane and Benjamin. They have served in various administrative, pastoral, and leadership positions. _Jim Hodges_ writes, "I believe God has so anointed them that they will leave a rich deposit of vision and revelation..."

David Shibley of Global Advance states, "...they will bring both challenge and encouragement to your people. They are indeed a cutting edge ministry for this hour."

"They are solid, reliable, extraordinarily competent people of rare vision and energy. I believe the Thompsons have much to share with the body of Christ in many places, near and far. Their special interest in and study of the New Testament church gives them an authentic voice for renewal and Biblical principles." The late _John Garlock; Garlock Ministries_.

Secondly, to answer the heart cry from around the world of: 'Give US leaders!' Global Leadership Network has developed over 200 hours of training seminars, conferences, consultation and curriculum. The emphasis is on five key areas: Leadership Principles, Life in the Spirit, Supportive Roles, Relational Principles, and Communication Principles. Global Leadership Network's desire is to mentor and equip leaders for the present task, as well as positioning for the 21st century.

Thirdly, is missions. Two-Thirds of the world is yet to be reached with the Good News of Jesus Christ. Global Leadership Network's mission focus is to go and train the national leaders by putting tried and true principles into their hands. At the same time, bring missionaries together for a time of ministry and refreshing. _Dick Mills_ writes, "In my observations, I've noticed their pulse and heartbeat for world missions." _Sam Farina of Sam Farina Ministries_ states, "Their overseas travels have been received with great recommendation and desire for more. I would say to you without hesitation, that I recommend them for the ministry, and I recommend what they are doing overseas as important and vital."

For Additional Copies of this Book, or other Media by the author, write to:

GLNM

P.O. Box 721

Montgomery, Texas 77356

E mail: www.terrylthompson.org

Amazon Kindle